This book contains
the medici[...]
Enjoy! Kay

· Carole
· Rita

A Tale of Two Biddies

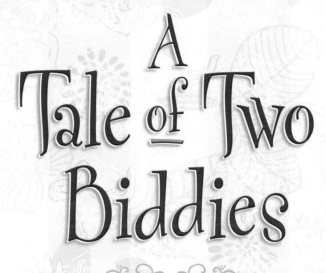

Vicki Kuyper

BroadStreet

PUBLISHING

Published by BroadStreet Publishing Group, LLC
Racine, Wisconsin, USA
www.broadstreetpublishing.com

A TALE of TWO BIDDIES

© 2015 by Vicki Kuyper

ISBN: 978-1-4245-5024-1 (hard cover)
ISBN: 978-1-4245-5053-1 (e-book)

No part of this book may be reproduced or transmitted in any form or by any means, except for brief quotations in printed reviews, without permission in writing from the publisher.

Scripture marked TPT is from The Passion Translation®, copyright © 2015 by BroadStreet Publishing Group, LLC, Racine, Wisconsin, USA. Used by permission. All rights reserved worldwide. www.thepassiontranslation.com. Scripture marked NIV is from THE HOLY BIBLE, NEW INTERNATIONAL VERSION®, NIV® Copyright © 1973, 1978, 1984, 2011 by Biblica, Inc.® Used by permission. All rights reserved worldwide. All Scripture marked NLT is from the Holy Bible, New Living Translation, copyright © 1996, 2004, 2007 by Tyndale House Foundation. Used by permission of Tyndale House Publishers, Inc., Carol Stream, Illinois 60188. All rights reserved.

Cover design by Chris Garborg at www.garborgdesign.com
Interior design and typesetting by Katherine Lloyd at www.theDESKonline.com

Stock or custom editions of BroadStreet Publishing titles may be purchased in bulk for educational, business, ministry, fundraising, or sales promotional use. For information, please e-mail info@broadstreetpublishing.com.

Printed in China

15 16 17 18 19 20   7 6 5 4 3 2 1

Dedicated to my grandmothers,
Kitty and Mardel,
as well as written in memory
of so many wonderful women
I've known and loved who never
had the opportunity
to open the gift of growing old:

Vereda Williams
Allysa Geske
Kristen Balsis
Doreen Buller
Pam Galliano
Julie Sawyer
Sandy Hopkins

CONTENTS

CHAPTER ONE

Meet the Biddies

O nce upon a time there lived two biddies. Of course, that wasn't the whole story. Just moments before, they'd been young mothers, new brides, giggling teens, teetering toddlers, and fragile infants opening their eyes to the wonders of this world for the very first time. Or at least that's how it seemed. But time passes. And so does every one of those marvelous stages of life.

Then comes stage "biddy." At first glance, maturity (that's the politically correct term for "going to pot," "over the hill," "past your prime," "long in the tooth," and other equally flattering euphemisms) looks like the ugly stepsister of life's phases. It brings to mind words like *menopause, colonoscopy, bone density,* and *Depends*.

Lucky us. No, really! In the early 1900s, most women didn't go through menopause. Why? Because they didn't live that long. Now, our average life span extends into the mid-80s. That's nearly forty additional years—almost an entire lifetime just one century ago. It's like winning those gold coins that give you an extra life in Super Mario Bros.* (Okay, so I played video games with my kids when they were young. I can still hear that annoying theme song in my head. So why can't I remember where I put my reading glasses? I digress…)

So our most pressing question as we enter these Mario Bros. golden bonus years is: How are we going to spend our extra life?

To help us answer that question in a personal, practical way, let's take a few lessons from two real-life biddies, Kitty and Mardel.

ST. KATHERINE AND THE DRAGON LADY

Grandmothers are like a church potluck. You never know what you're going to get. God blessed me with two women at opposite ends of the Biddy Spectrum. Kitty was the grandmother everyone wanted to call their own. She was kind, tenderhearted, humble, and followed Jesus so closely that she died at noon on Good Friday.

In contrast, Mardel was a loose cannon—critical, pessimistic, self-centered, and sharp tongued. All of which earned her the family moniker of "Dragon Lady." Blind in one eye, she'd barrel her sky-blue Cadillac out of her driveway, in reverse, honking her way into oncoming traffic. She simply assumed everyone would stop for her. I think that's kind of how she felt about life in general.

She lived to be ninety-six. But apparently that wasn't long enough for her to learn my children's names. All two of them. She simply referred to her only grandchildren as "Vicki's boy-child" and "Vicki's girl-child," as if they were characters right out of the pages of *The Jungle Book*. It's not as though my husband and I named them Mowgli and Rumpelstiltskin. "Ryan" and "Katrina" didn't seem all that tricky to master.

Then again, maybe it was Mardel's way of getting back at us for naming Katrina after Grandma Kitty. Not that we ever told her. We figured that if we used Katrina instead of Katherine, we could let Grandma Kitty know we were honoring her while Mardel would be none the wiser. Perhaps I underestimated the homing device of Mardel's intuition.

Not that it was always on target. One time she misplaced a Christmas tin filled with old hair curlers. She was convinced the neighbor who'd dropped by for a visit earlier that day had absconded with them when using the bathroom. What a ruse! Did I mention her neighbor was an elderly bald man?

Of course, Mardel didn't become Dragon Lady overnight. Like all of us, there's more to her story than just her biddy years. Mardel grew up on a small ranch in California. Horses, guns, and lots of hard work were the "toys" of her childhood. In her early teenage years, her brother's rifle misfired out in the front yard. The bullet came through a window into the house, hitting Mardel in the eye. She spent months in a dark room, recuperating from her injury.

Despite her accident, Mardel remained an avid sharp-shooter and hunter. As a kid, I listened to her and my grandfather regale countless tales about deer hunting in Nevada's Ruby Mountains. My favorite was how she shot and dressed a deer (for those of you who do not have a deer-hunting grandmother, that means she cut out its internal organs, not that she decked it out in a cocktail frock and pumps). Then Mardel made my mother (who had never camped or hunted before, let alone seen an animal butchered right before her eyes) carry the warm liver back to camp in her hat.

This memorable little episode took place on my parents' honeymoon. So much for romance.

Long story short, Grandma Mardel was a rough-and-tumble sort of gal. She liked to smoke (back in the day when smoking was cool), gamble, hang out with the guys, and wear ostentatious, fake jewels and anything-but-fake furs. Her favorite place to be was squarely in the center of attention.

In contrast, Grandma Kitty was a self-proclaimed wall-flower. Painfully shy, she fretted over her lack of schooling, social graces, and red hair. (The latter of which Kitty passed on to me, for which I'm grateful.)

Raised in a very strict home, Kitty followed suit by

marrying a jealous, controlling man. But back in high school another young man was "sweet" on her. Kitty often retold the story of how he surprised her one day with a beautiful bouquet. But when Kitty returned home from school the next day, her flowers were nowhere to be seen. Her stepmother told her she'd visited the cemetery that morning and took them to place on a relative's grave.

Seventy years later, I still don't think my grandmother ever got over the fate of those flowers. That's as far as the story of her would-be beau ever went. But Kitty and I wrote lots of new stories together, particularly after I entered adulthood.

When I got engaged, I asked her to be a bridesmaid in my wedding—enticing her with the promise of walking down the aisle on the arm of a handsome young grooms-man. True to form, she blushed, giggled, and politely declined, but said she'd always treasure the fact that she'd been asked.

Other than lamenting that waylaid bouquet, and the fact that her "real" mother died when she was young, I rarely heard a word of complaint from Kitty—until dementia took hold in her late eighties. (Even then, when she was thinking clearly she'd apologize for anything she'd said or done that might have been unseemly, all of it uncharacteristic and unremembered.) As for Mardel, "woe is me" could have been her middle name.

Kitty was widowed in her early sixties. Mardel, a few

years later. Kitty lived in a one-bedroom apartment on a meager income. Mardel lived in a nice home in the hills and had money to burn. Kitty and Mardel were both women of faith, though their Catholic faith looked different on each of them. Kitty attended mass every morning and worked as a church secretary well into her seventies. Mardel went to mass on Christmas and Easter and fused her faith in God with mysticism and superstition.

As these two women aged and their inhibitions fell away, the true character of their hearts became increasingly apparent to those around them. For better or for worse. Was it nature, nurture, or their very own choices that shaped the legacy of St. Katherine and the Dragon Lady?

The answer is "all of the above." That means we each have some control over who we'll be when we grow up—and grow old. So, while we still have all (or at least some!) of our mental faculties about us, we'd better make a decision as to which direction we want to go.

BIDDY IN TRAINING

Not all biddies are created equal. A "biddy" can be a chicken or a cleaning woman. It can be a nickname for Bridget. In Australia, it's a two-for-one fast-food voucher. But the biddies we're focusing on right now are you and me. We're both biddies in training. One of us may be ahead of the other in terms of age, but if God has bestowed on us the privilege of laugh lines, a glacially paced metabolism, and chin hairs that have started sprouting like tulips after a winter thaw, we're well on our way toward biddydom.

So we'd better start planning now.

We grow old in the blink of an eye. However, growing up takes considerably longer. Some of us never really do, even though we live into our eighties and beyond. That's because growing up involves maturing, and maturing involves change. And change is hard.

We like our ruts. We eat the same thing for breakfast. Hang out with the same friends. Wear the same mom jeans we wore when our children were young—if we're lucky enough to not have bumped up the waist size a time or two. Our favorite songs are the same ones we played on our car radio back when those bands were actually on top of the charts instead of touting their fourth Farewell Reunion Tour.

Ruts can be our friends. Chances are if we've always been active, we still are. If we've always eaten healthy, we still do. If we've maintained a strong faith, loving relationships, and a healthy self-image, we're probably still following these same positive ruts forward into the future.

But what if the ruts we've worn into our lives are leading us somewhere we never intended to go? What if we're selfish, mean spirited, and cynical? Not that we see ourselves that way. What we see when we look in the mirror may be an independent, truth-telling realist. Of course, if we need reading glasses to decipher a price tag, perhaps the way we see ourselves has also grown a bit fuzzy over time. We may be way past due for an "I" check.

Who are we … really?

The older we get, the more stuck in our ruts we become. That means there's no better time to reevaluate our habits, our worth, our faith, and our future than right now. If we've got a whole new bonus life ahead of us, let's choose to spend it well! Trade in that Bucket List for a Becoming List.

What kind of biddy do we want to become?

CHOOSE LIFE

Getting older is a privilege. It's a gift not everyone receives. So how do we accept it with open arms and enjoy it with a hopeful heart in spite of the challenges it brings our way?

Deuteronomy 30:19 says, "I have set before you life and death, blessings and curses. Now choose life" (NIV). We can't control the aging process. But we do have a choice as to how we're going to face each day that comes our way. Each choice we make helps shape our heart as well as our life—and our bonus life. We can choose what draws us closer to God and closer to becoming the women God created us to be. That's life at its finest.

But the choice is up to us. Just ask my mom.

My mother, following in the footsteps of her mother, Kitty, excels at choosing life. More than a decade ago, she had a series of life-threatening strokes. After awaking from a coma, she had to relearn to swallow, eat, walk, read, and so much more. Every day was a challenge. She spent months in a rehabilitation hospital, many more months recovering at home, and years continuing to slowly regain most of the abilities she'd lost.

Now in her eighties, my mom takes line-dancing classes, goes to the gym, and loves to travel. Just a few months ago, we flew to London to take a transatlantic cruise, just the two of us. Mom said when she told her friends at The Village (her retirement community) about her upcoming trip, not one of them wanted to go. As a matter of fact, she said they really weren't interested in going any farther than The Village's front door.

"They're alive," she said, "but they're already dead."

She was so right. We choose life, or death, every day. So, fellow biddy, which will you choose today?

CHAPTER TWO

The Wizard of Uhs...

omeone keeps trying to hack into my online accounts. Unfortunately, that person is me. Passwords, pin codes, and occasionally the names of my very own children are just a few of the informational black holes created by my aging brain. But it's more than just names and numbers that disappear. Tangible objects have been known to go missing.

One Christmas not so long ago, my sweet daughter gave my hubby and me tickets to see Les Mis. As the performance date drew near, I wanted to check the time the curtain went up. I rifled through my Important Stuff file folder. The tickets were nowhere to be found. I checked my desk drawer. My purse. Assorted piles of paper on countertops and nightstands. My underwear drawer. The vegetable crisper. Nothing. I concluded we must have thrown them away in the flurry of gift wrap after Christmas. Sheepishly, we paid the replacement fee and went on to enjoy the show.

Months passed. Easter was now just around the corner. Time to make deviled eggs. I took out the cake decorator I use to pipe the yolk into fluffy yellow peaks. (Don't be too impressed. It's one of the few family recipes I make that doesn't wind up looking like Pinterest "fail" photos.) What should I find in the box? You guessed it. Two tickets to Les Mis. Okay, so I did make deviled eggs over the Christmas/New Years holiday. But exactly how those tickets traveled from our living room to the kitchen and then into the decorator box remains a menopausal mystery. All I can say is I must have gotten distracted on the way to my Important Stuff folder.

Not as though that's a big surprise. These days I can't take a shower and mentally organize my day at the same time. Just last week, I caught myself washing my face with my hair conditioner instead of facial scrub. At least now the hair on my upper lip seems shinier and more full bodied.

Honestly, I used to be a whiz at multitasking, absolutely undistractible. I could carry on a phone conversation while writing on my computer with music blaring in the background as I also sipped tea and snacked on cookies. These days, if the heater happens to click on while I'm working, I get so distracted I need a cookie break and head to the kitchen, where I notice I haven't cleaned out the dishwasher, which then gets halfway emptied before I see a birthday card I forgot to mail on the counter, but before I can head out to the mailbox my phone alerts me to a text from someone asking if we're still meeting for lunch—where I was supposed to be fifteen minutes ago. Of course to read the text I try to put on a pair of reading glasses only to discover I'm already wearing one.

Yes, times have changed and so has my brain. Why? Aging has ushered me into a second adolescence. My face is breaking out. My monthly cycle's out of whack. My hormones are as jumpy as an over-caffeinated assassin. I have work that needs to be done, an ever-growing to-do list hovering over me, making me sweat (or is that a hot flash?). But all I can muster any interest in is losing myself between the pages of a novel or reposting Facebook videos of kittens singing with the dubbed voices of celebrity pop stars. What's a biddy to do?

The first time I hit adolescence, I couldn't wait to be older. Now, I dream of what it was like to be younger. Thinner. Prettier. Quicker on my feet. Quicker in my recall. If I can't have a younger body, I'll settle for a younger brain. *My* brain. The one that actually worked. The one that was fun to go out with because it remembered the punch line to the joke I'm in the middle of telling. The one that could locate car keys, theater tickets, and the parking space I pulled my car into less than ten minutes ago. The one that attracted minutia like my black dress pants collect lint. The one that made me feel smart.

If my brain weren't such an indistinguishably unattractive blob of gray matter, I'd post its picture on a milk carton. *LOST: My mind. Reward offered if returned in condition I last saw it, sometime in my mid-40s.* Unfortunately, countless other women of a certain age would be convinced it was their very own misplaced marbles. There'd be custody battles. Catfights—and those cats would probably be crooning "Let It Go." Hold on a minute while I check Facebook…

ADOLESCENCE IS BETTER THE SECOND TIME AROUND

Now, where was I? Oh, yeah…adolescence. It's not just for kids anymore. As we head through perimenopause (the ten years or so that precede menopause) our brains are enacting a geriatric version of Hormones Gone Wild. In direct opposition to our first adolescence, now our estrogen and testosterone (it's not just for men!) levels are plummeting, along with our thyroid levels. This plays havoc with things like our memory, our ability to multitask, and the speed with which we process new information. Not to mention the speed with which our body processes the calories of the cookies we just ate!

Believe it or not, just as our metabolism slows to a glacial pace, our brain's response to glucose also goes haywire. This causes our energy levels to yo-yo up and down, which triggers cravings for more sweets and carbs.[1] I guess

---

1   Louann Brizendine, MD, *The Female Brain* (New York: Three Rivers Press, 2006), 140.

the good news would be that our brains are shrinking by about .05 percent each year, so at we're least losing some weight—in our cranium.[2]

Great. So, we're walking around in a mental fog and acquiring the waistline of a sumo wrestler. But wait, there's more! Like teenagers, we're also undergoing an identity crisis.

Back when we only had to deal with PMS (kind of like perimenopause with training wheels), estrogen broke our monthly cycles down into three distinct emotional and physical phases. Just before ovulation, estrogen helped direct our mental and physical energy outward toward what was going on around us. We were busy, focused, and productive. During ovulation, we felt pretty good about life and connected especially well relationally with others. During our premenstrual phase (when PMS reared its not-so-attractive head), we were more likely to be out of sorts with the outside world because our thoughts and energy were directed inward.

As we enter the Biddy Years, we get stuck in this pseudo-PMS phase for weeks or months at a time. We become more introspective. We weigh who we are against who we want to be. We do the same with the world, as our minds actually become more responsive to perceived injustice and inequality.[3] For some this can be a midlife crisis. For others it can spark a midlife genesis. It all depends on what

---

2 Martha Weinman Lear, *Where Did I Leave My Glasses?* (New York: Wellness Central, Hachette Book Group, 2009), 7.

3 Christiane Northrup, MD, *The Wisdom of Menopause* (New York: Bantam Books, 2006), 19.

we choose to do with the insight our changing brain helps reveal to us.

One thing we can choose to do is follow the advice of Romans 12:2, "Do not conform to the pattern of this world, but be transformed by the renewing of your mind. Then you will be able to test and approve what God's will is—his good, pleasing and perfect will" (NIV). What old age will look like on you and me doesn't have to conform to any pattern or stereotype we've seen in the past. How we live out God's good, pleasing, and perfect will in the Biddy Years will be our own one-of-a-kind adventure. Who knows? Perhaps our newfound sensitivity to repression, prejudice, and inequity is simply another way our minds are being renewed to better reflect God's image—and guide us through the season ahead.

THE OLD GRAY MATTER...
SHE AIN'T WHAT SHE USED TO BE

Obviously, this whole aging brain thing is a mixed bag of cerebral ups and downs. Word on the street (supported by recent research) promises that after menopause winds up, our brains will settle down and our memory will level out a bit. That doesn't mean we'll morph back into a twenty-year-old multitasking whiz, but at least we won't burst into tears as easily when we misplace our bra.

It's up to us to become proactive in helping our biddy brains keep up with the fast pace of life. How? We can step up our own pace by going for a brisk walk. By now, it isn't news to any of us that exercise benefits our body. That includes our brain. In a study funded by the National Institute of Aging, participants who walked at least six miles a week had a 50 percent lower risk of developing memory problems. The average age of participants was seventy-eight![4]

Even though our brains are shrinking, aerobic exercise helps preserve—and can even increase—the amount of gray matter we have in our hippocampus and prefrontal cortex, regions related to memory. It also generates a chemical called BDNF, which helps us learn new skills.[5] Add a bit of strength training and a low-fat, low-cholesterol diet, and we can help protect our biddy brains against dementia while sprouting a few new brain cells along the way.

"But what about crossword puzzles?" you may ask. "Can't I exercise my brain while snacking on the couch?" Well, there are benefits to doing crossword puzzles and so-called brain training exercises. Every time we get an answer right, our brain gets a little zap of dopamine, which makes us feel good. We may even pick up a few memorization techniques along the way. But puzzles do nothing to physically change our brains for the better. If you enjoy them, do them. Just remember to go for a walk once you've put that pencil down.

So we can choose to exercise, eat right, and enjoy a few

---

4   Ava Feuer, "The Latest Science on Aging," *Oprah* magazine, May 2012.
5   Lear, *Where Did I Leave My Glasses?*, 58.

puzzles along the way. We can choose to be transformed instead of conform. But something else we have the power to choose is our attitude toward the years ahead. Remember Grandma Mardel, alias Dragon Lady? We can choose to be like her, continually griping about getting older. Or, we can choose to roll with the punches and laugh at ourselves, like Grandma Kitty did when she hid the eggs for the Easter egg hunt and no one could find them. Not even her.

If we expect our Biddy Years to be a miserable downhill slog through the mud, chances are we'll experience them that way. However, if we choose to anticipate a season of newfound growth, adventure, and a lot of laughs, chances are good it will live up to our expectations.

That means when I find tickets in the cake decorator box or comment to my husband at Target, "Isn't this a cool coffee pot?" and he responds, "Why, yes it is; though some people call it a 'Crock-Pot,'" I will laugh and accept the fact that this old gray matter ain't what she used to be. And that's okay. The rest of me isn't the same gal I was at twenty either. And I'm grateful.

Sure, I'm older. But I really am wiser. I'm richer in the things that matter most and more content with the life God's set before me. My biddy brain taught me that. And in the coming years, I'm certain I'll be able to see God's big picture even more clearly. At least I will if I can track down those reading glasses...

CHAPTER THREE

The Long and Whiney Road

I t's a day that will live on in infamy, a menopausal melt-down of epic proportions. On Mother's Day, no less. And it's all because of "mindful eating." Well, that and the fact that the estrogen levels in my body were plummeting like a skydiver whose chute refused to open. Unfortunately, that chute was comprised of maturity, logic, and self-control—and it was undeniably AWOL.

My task seemed simple enough. All I had to do was introduce the speaker at church that morning. Since I hadn't met her personally, I went to her website to familiarize myself with her work. There it was: mindful eating. That means actually engaging your brain before shoving something in your mouth, asking yourself questions like, "Am I am really hungry?"

That's all it took to send me into a full-scale biddy

blowup. I embarked on a teary-eyed diatribe about the incredible insensitivity of preaching to mothers on Mother's Day about how they should think about what they eat right before they head out to the one and only buffet they enjoy once a year in honor of all the sacrifices they make, including carrying a child the size of a small planet on their bladder for nine months and then pushing that heavenly body through their nether regions, not to mention breastfeeding, potty training, disciplining, carpooling, and putting up with all of the *&$@*# they dish out for eighteen years and beyond!

Let's pause here for just a moment. If you don't know me personally, I want to assure you I'm generally a rather levelheaded gal. I rarely get angry and never, ever swear. Which is why I watched my husband and adult daughter, who witnessed this catastrophic event firsthand, go from being horrified to trying to control their hysterical laughter. Wisely, they surmised that if they started guffawing aloud, my sights would shift from mindful eating to mindfully shredding my own family members.

The truth is, I was as horrified and amused as they were. It was like I was trapped inside this crazy woman, watching her make a complete idiot of herself, and there was not a thing I could do to stop her. When my mouth finally ran out of steam, I just stood there. Stunned into silence. Then, I freshened my makeup, went to church, graciously introduced the speaker (at least that's what it looked like from the outside), smoldered under the conviction of her perfectly reasonable message, and then ate like there was no tomorrow at my Mother's Day buffet.

Consider yourself warned. Menopause can awaken the sleeping dragon in all of us. Well, all of us women, anyway. Aren't we the lucky ones?

BID ADIEU TO ESTROGEN

For so many years, estrogen has been our faithful friend. This lovely little group of hormones gave us curves and enabled us to give birth. It preserved our bone strength, regulated our liver's production of cholesterol, kept our hair strong and full, played a role in clotting our blood, helped protect our nervous system, encouraged serotonin and endorphins (the "feel good" chemicals) to course through our brains, kept our skin stretchy, our body temperature consistent, and our moods on a fairly predictable monthly cycle of ups and downs. Perhaps we never gave estrogen the fanfare it truly deserved. Alas, it's too late now.

Throughout our body there are little receptors that respond to estrogen. This is why when we enter perimenopause (the stage where estrogen begins its long, drawn-out farewell, which reaches its crescendo in menopause) our whole body feels the effects. Well, most of us do, anyway. About one third of women have no perimenopausal symptoms that disrupt their quality of life.[1] To those of you who

1 Cary Barbor, "Not Your Mother's Menopause," *More* magazine, March 2008.

fit into this category all I have to say is, "How does it feel to be one of God's chosen few?"

As for the rest of us, calling this season of life "the change" is an understatement. It's more like Invasion of the Body Snatchers. We've already seen what's happening to our poor, little biddy brains. A bit later, we'll take a closer look at bonuses like weight gain and age spots. (Oh, goodie! Something to look forward to!) But there's still so much more we have to explore.

First, there's the fact that we can now create our very own microclimate. For me, the onset of perimenopause coincided with my move to Arizona. Needless to say, hot flashes in Phoenix are redundant. These lovely little power surges cause us to rip off layers of clothing, and then put them back on, like a high-speed version of strip poker. On the average, we can expect this little game to continue for 10.2 years.[2] And we don't just play it during the day.

Night sweats can wreak havoc on a good night's sleep. But since our estrogen loss also jump-starts insomnia, chances are we haven't enjoyed one of those in quite a while. It's no wonder ZzzQuil™ and I have recently become such fast friends. One small swig of the big Z ensures that at least a few brains cells will be rested and functioning come daybreak. Since I've been a teetotaler all my life, this is the closest I get to a cocktail. I reassure myself with the knowledge that this sleep aid is non-habit-forming and that

2 "Body and Mind" column, *More* magazine, December 2011/January 2012, 136.

a little red wine in the evening is supposed to be good for you. However, not being a wine connoisseur, I'm unclear if its "warming berry flavor" leans more toward a cabernet or a merlot.

But even a sleep aid can't stop my aging bladder (and the muscles supporting it) from getting me up to heed nature's call several times a night. As for the daylight hours, I make sure I know where a restroom is at all times. Just in case. Luckily there's biddy-bladder–friendly technology out there to help me. Yes, there's an app for that. Check out WhereToWee.com if you need to find the closest restroom. At a movie? RunPee.com will let you know the best time to sneak out without missing a major plot point.

A much-lower-tech asset we're forced to rely on during the Biddy Years is reading glasses. We finally understand why those old ladies of yesteryear kept their glasses on chains around their necks. Sure, they needed to keep them close at hand to read a price tag, a menu, their watch, or to tell them which side of the book was "up." But that chain also reduces the risk of having to put on a pair of readers to locate the pair you just put down a minute ago. This new-found dependency is caused by the ciliary muscle in our eyes losing its flexibility, which happens sometime between our thirty-eighth and forty-fifth birthday.

But that's not the only flexibility we lose. Remember the Ten-Second Rule, where if you dropped a perfectly good cookie onto a relatively clean floor you could still eat it if you picked it up in less than ten seconds? That's been replaced by the Ten-Minute Biddy Rule. If we drop a cookie—or a quarter or a Q-tip or a book or our reading glasses—and go to pick them up but can't get back to a standing position in less than ten minutes, we promise to ask for a Medic Alert necklace for Christmas. Or we can simply kick the cookie, etc., under a nearby counter and forget about it. After all, just getting out of bed some mornings can feel like we're living *50 Shades of Bengay.*

Of course, not all of the changes we're experiencing affect how we feel physically. Others affect how we feel about ourselves. Take our hair, for instance. 1 Corinthians 11:15 talks about a woman's hair being her "glory." These days, old glory is looking pretty tarnished. Not only is it turning gray, it seems to be the only part of our body hell-bent on getting thin. At least we have options. We can dye it and start taking styling tips from Donald Trump.

What's weird is that the fewer hairs that sprout from the top of our head, the more that begin to show up in places we never expected. (I'm proud to say I can now grow a better mustache than most teenage boys I know.) Instead of a bikini wax, we can now spend our money waxing our chins and our toes.

Besides looking like a yeti, we begin to act like one as well. (See aforementioned Mother's Day saga.) There are plenty of apps that track menstrual cycles and their corresponding PMS-related mood swings (some of them even send text alerts to warn family members of impending meltdowns), but unfortunately, nothing can track the unpredictable cycles of perimenopause. I've found the two things that work best for me are going on vacation or wearing white pants. Either of these will cause my menses, which has been in abstention for months, to reappear with a vengeance.

Truth be told, this is what menopause is really all about—when our menses pause. Well, they're actually supposed to stop. Or that's what I hear. But mine keep hitting the pause button over and over again, then surprising me at the most inopportune times. The average age for women to go through menopause is 51.5 years. About 5 percent of women experience early menopause, between the ages of 40 and 45. Another 5 percent go through late menopause, after the age of 55.[3]

I am 58 and counting. I've always been an overachiever. I guess God wanted to provide me with enough time and material to write this book. Considering how graciously He's blessed me in my life, I'll probably be one of the 5 to 10 percent of women who continue having hot flashes beyond the age of 70. Think of the money I'll save on heating.

When we talk about menopause, we're actually talking about only one day. It's the day that marks one year since our last period. Like a convenience store the night before

---

3 "Menopause," The Center for Menstrual Disorders and Reproductive Choice, http://www.cmdrc.com/middle-to-transition-years/menopause.

Easter, it's when we run completely out of eggs. That's when we officially graduate from perimenopause to being meno-pausal. I still have four months until that one-year mark. But I leave on vacation tomorrow. Who knows? The count-down could start all over again.

THE REAL 24

Did you ever watch the TV show *24*? Each season follows CIA agent Jack Bauer through one terrible, horrible, no good, very bad day. I'd like to see Jack face those twenty-four hours after suffering through a decade of sleep deprivation, absentmindedness, compromised eyesight, bone density loss, hot flashes, menstrual cramps, and mood swings. Chances are that by then he'd either have dropped out of sight or he'd be ready to face just about anything.

We have that same choice. Whether we're perimeno-pausal, menopausal, or still clinging tightly to our estrogen in anticipation of the potentially rocky road that lies ahead, we're all given the same twenty-four hours. (Unlike Jack, hopefully they're devoid of any bombs threats, car chases, or terrorist plots!) If we're blessed, we'll receive the gift of another 1,440 minutes tomorrow. But there are no guar-antees. All we have to work with is the here and now. This minute only comes around once. We can use it or lose it, embrace it or waste it.

Ecclesiastes 3:1 says, "There is a time for everything, and a season for every activity under the heavens" (NIV). Okay, so we're in a challenging season. Verse two continues, "a time to be born and a time to die." We're not dead yet!

Remember Grandma Kitty and Mardel? I have no idea how they handled perimenopause. First, because I was a mere egg when their last egg bid them farewell. Secondly, because no one back then really talked about "female problems" of that nature. Even during my mother's generation, I heard only faint whispers about "the change."

We're part of a new generation. Candid, even intimate, topics are no longer considered taboo among family and friends. They may even be shared from the pulpit on Sunday mornings. In the media, we're bombarded with issues like menstrual cycles, ED, birth control, and vaginal dryness. While we may cringe when we see our kids and grandkids exposed to topics we'd rather not have to explain quite yet, the upside is information is readily available to us. That includes information on menopause.

I know you'd love for me to tell you exactly what to do to help you better bid estrogen adieu. To tell you to go with bioidenticals or black cohosh or acupuncture. To fight hot flashes by cutting down on caffeine and sugar, pumping up your exercise routine, or adding more strawberries, peppers, and salad greens to your diet. To stock up on ZzzQuil. To do nothing more than grin and bear it. All of these are valid options. But there are so many more.

God created each of our bodies with its own unique menopausal season. What works for me may not be best for you. So talk to your doctor. Do some research on your own. Talk to friends about what they've found helpful. Ask God for wisdom in choosing the right road. Then walk it.

A Gallup survey showed that more than half of American women between the ages of fifty and sixty-five felt this was the happiest and most fulfilling season of their lives.[4] Will you be one of them?

Once again, it comes down to choices. Today is a once-in-a-lifetime opportunity. It may contain hot flashes and hormones gone wild, but if that's all we're focused on, we'll miss out on everything else. And there's always so much more. Let's open the gift of today like kids at a birthday party, filled with anticipation, excitement, and a belief that anything can happen. With God, it can.

---

4   Christiane Northrup, MD, *The Wisdom of Menopause* (New York: Bantam Books, 2006), 6.

CHAPTER FOUR

She Ain't Heavy, She's My Mother

Friends often tell my son he looks like Spongebob Squarepants. Of course, I've also heard how much my son looks just like me. Draw your own conclusions.

The good news is I'm half the woman I used to be. Well, maybe three-fourths would be more accurate. In my early twenties, I spent my junior year of college studying in Florence, Italy—where I lived above a bakery. When I returned home ten months later, I carried an extra forty pounds of Italian pasta and baked goods with me. And they weren't in my suitcase.

But I was young. I took up running and cut down on sweets. I lost twenty pounds in six months. Then I fell in love. The next twenty pounds just kind of disappeared on their own.

I can still remember lathering up in the shower one

morning when my elbow hit something pointy. Imagine my surprise to discover my very own hipbone! I felt like an archaeologist who'd uncovered buried treasure.

That was then. Perimenopause is now. Once again, my hipbones have gone into hiding. But they're not alone. According to the International Menopause Society, nine out of ten perimenopausal and menopausal women will gain weight, averaging ten to twenty pounds. Even worse news, 95 percent of menopausal women who diet will regain two-thirds of the weight they've lost within one year. Within five years, they will regain virtually all of it.

I suppose the good news is that our pelvic bones don't stop expanding until we're seventy, adding as much as three more inches to our midsection than we had in our twenties. So, in theory, my hipbones should now be easier to find. Lucky me.

Yes, we've reached that magical time of life when we can eat less, exercise more, and still gain weight. And that weight starts showing up in the weirdest places. Who would have guessed that my back would one day need its own girdle? Or that my once-flat stomach could grow a menopot overnight? Not that it isn't handy now and then. Who needs one of those fancy little pillows to balance your book, e-reader, or glass of iced tea when you have your very own belly bolster? I'm just thankful I never had my navel pierced, because by now that little bauble would have gone subterranean.

So, with our metabolism slowing to that of a three-toed sloth, is there anything we can do other than watch our bodies slowly morph into the shape of a garden gnome? Actually there is. And we all know what it is. We just don't want to do it.

EXERCISE?
I THOUGHT YOU SAID, "ACCESSORIZE!"

I've never been one of those waiflike women with a body fat ratio equal to that of a praying mantis. The ones who can wear yoga pants out in public without first donning a pair of industrial-strength shapewear. When I work out (and yes, I actually do!), I look like I need it. And even though I've been pretty consistent at trying to make physical activity part of my new and improved Biddy Rut for the last three years, I'm still far from looking like a model. Unless, of course, you're picturing a Model T.

I also don't enjoy it. My husband, on the other hand, would spend his entire life at the gym if he didn't have to actually make money to pay for his membership. He considers lifting weights, going to spin class, and having a personal trainer push him beyond what he thinks he can do—*fun*. Did I mention he "enjoys" all of this before the sun comes up?

Luckily, I have a medical condition I can use as my Get Out Of Gym Free Card. I get exercise-induced migraines. And no, this isn't a made-up psychosomatic excuse. My friends all pushed me to try yoga, assuring me I'd feel wonderful afterward. Downward dog made me feel as sick as one. I tried a free gym membership but needed Dramamine just to run on the treadmill. And, of course, who wouldn't have a headache after trying to squeeze into a spandex bra top in a gym locker room? I felt like a bratwurst trying to shimmy into the casing of a cocktail weenie.

So, what did I do? I kept trying until I found something I *could* do. A friend opened a Pilates studio in her home. She worked with me to build a routine that doesn't make me feel like I'm riding a Tilt-A-Whirl. I go twice a week. Do I love it? No. But I don't hate it. Best of all, I'm stronger, have better balance, and my jiggly underarms (or "bingo wings" as they're affectionately known across the pond) are a little less jiggly than they were three years ago.

Both of my grandmothers had free-flying bingo wings as far back as I can remember. Back in the day, you just covered them up and tried not to wave too vigorously. Kitty was shaped like a number-two pencil and Mardel like a squat, round eraser. But both of them lived into their nineties with very few health problems.

Kitty never got her driver's license and walked everywhere—to work, to the store, or to the bus stop if her destination was farther than her feet could carry her. Into her eighties, she could keep pace with her great-grandkids. But once Kitty became more sedentary, she soon became less steady on her feet and considerably more frail. At ninety-three, her body was in relatively good health when she fell getting out of the car and broke her hip. She died a week later.

Our takeaway? Keep moving. Research has shown that women who exercise regularly live an average of six years longer than those who don't.[1] Why gyp our bonus life out of six extra years? And we don't have to be gym rats to reap the benefits. (Unless, of course, you and my husband are kindred spirits!) What was your favorite way to "move" when you were young? Tennis? So what if you can no longer rock that itty-bitty tennis skirt! Sweats will do. Just pick up your racket and go hit some balls. Even if you miss them, you'll get some exercise chasing them around the court.

Maybe you loved dancing. Try Zumba. Can't afford it or don't want to drive across town? Crank up your favorite tunes and boogie around the living room. Preferably with the blinds closed. Want to add a little weight-bearing exercise? Pick up your grandkid as a dance partner. No grandkids? Cut a rug with the cat.

Speaking of cats, following Grandma Kitty's lead and going for a walk is also an incredibly convenient, beneficial new rut to work into our routine. Walking thirty to forty-five minutes at least five times a week has been shown to make us happier, healthier, and a little less jiggly. But if that

---

1 Christiane Northrup, MD, *The Wisdom of Menopause* (New York: Bantam Books, 2001), 420.

sounds like a marathon right now, do what you can. Even five minutes of walking is better than another five minutes watching crime dramas on TV with a bag of chips balanced on your menopot.

We've already seen how walking benefits our brains, but it also helps firm up our buns and belly bolster. And as we build muscle, our metabolism gets kicked up a notch. Sure, walking may only push it from sloth to garden-snail speed, but every little bit helps. And since more muscle burns more calories and helps stabilize our blood sugar, it means that through our Biddy Years we don't have to subsist on lettuce and water. We can actually add a tomato.

RELAXED IS THE NEW SKINNY

Food is yummy. Well, lots of it is. I hold fast to the belief that if the tree of the knowledge of good and evil in the garden of Eden had sprouted broccoli instead of fruit, we'd still be living in paradise. No temptation there. At least not without a cheese sauce bush nearby.

I've long been a very vocal broccoli hater. But at this point in my life I should actually give it another try. There's a biological reason for this, not just good-natured chutzpah. Our ability to taste bitterness declines with the onset of menopause.[2] Since it's the bitterness of vegetables that

2 Amanda Greene, "7 Things You Didn't Know About Your Tastebuds," *Woman's Day*, February 8, 2013; www.nutritionist-resource.org.uk/blog/2013/02/08/how-our-tastes-change-with-age/.

usually leads people to shun them, I figure there's a chance that the few I don't already like may actually be palatable to me now.

But really, why bother? There are so many other wonderful things to eat. Like salted caramel cupcakes, green chili cheeseburgers, homemade mac and cheese, and chocolate-covered anything (well, maybe not broccoli). Wash it all down with an extra-large Dr. Pepper and call it lunch.

You can see the problem here…

Food is fuel. What we eat determines how well our body functions as well as what size jeans we wear. As we age and our bodies become less forgiving, we need to upgrade to a higher quality of fuel. Just like a fine sports car. I find it's helpful to picture myself as a former Ford Pinto who's been upgraded to a Porsche. But unless Porsche begins manufacturing minivans, I need to pay attention to the quantity of food I consume as well as the quality.

Over the years, I'd come to believe that the easiest diet advice for me would be: if it tastes good, spit it out. But that's no way to live. Like I said, food is yummy.

Interestingly enough, the diet I've found that works best for me is the Cruise Diet. Every time I go on a cruise, I lose weight. I know, this sounds like some kind of scam. But it's true. And trust me, I don't just nibble on salads at the buffet. I have my fair share of desserts. But I don't overeat. I'm active during the day. I eat very little processed food. Best of all, on a cruise I'm relaxed and having a wonderful time.

Believe it or not, it's the "relaxed and having a wonderful time" part that may be the most beneficial. Our bodies have two different nervous system modes. One is fight-or-flight. The other is rest-and-relax. Only one of these two systems can operate at a time. When we're stressed, overworked, overtired, anxious about the future (or even our appearance), our fight-or-flight mode is automatically switched on. This creates hormones like cortisol. Cortisol increases our blood sugar, helps us store fat, and makes us crave higher calorie foods. It's trying to do us a favor, working hard to prepare us for the impending apocalypse. But more often than not, that apocalypse is bigger in our mind than it is in real life.

Switching from fight-or-flight to rest-and-relax can take a major Biddy Rut shift. But it's worth it. It can help us lose weight without dieting as well as squeeze more joy out of our bonus years. Dieting on its own isn't a new, helpful rut. It's more like a bump in the road, a temporary change. Once we lose the weight, it's easy to slip right back into the same, familiar rut of eating habits we've traveled most of our lives. What we need is to forge a new, deep, healthy lifestyle rut.

Remember when I mentioned how twenty pounds just seemed to fall off when I was young and in love? That worked on the same principle as the Cruise Diet. The better we feel about ourselves and the world around us, the more our bodies relax, produce serotonin (which makes us feel happy), and store less fat.[3] We also don't feel the need

3   Martha Beck, "The Easier Way to Diet," *Oprah* magazine, June 2009.

to devour that whole plate of brownies. We can be satisfied with just one.

Of course not every day of our Biddy Years will feel like a carefree honeymoon cruise. Our current circumstances may switch on that fight-or-flight mode with good reason. That's when we need to do what we can and let God take care of the rest. I know that sounds like a trite little greeting card sentiment. But why should we let what we don't have any control over steal our peace of mind *and* make us fat?

Jesus said, "I am leaving you with a gift—peace of mind and heart. And the peace I give is a gift the world cannot give. So don't be troubled or afraid" (John 14:27 NLT).

We have access to Someone who can help us flip our fight-or-flight mode to rest-and relax. So let's make a biddy pact. When life hands us lemons, let's make lemon bars. We'll do what we can. Then we'll go for a walk (as a gift to ourselves and our metabolism) and talk to Jesus about what stresses us out. We'll contemplate His gift of peace.

And one more thing…we'll refuse to judge our worth, or our beauty, by a number on the scale or the tag on our jeans. We'll rest in who we are right here, right now. Bingo wings and all.

CHAPTER FIVE

Seniorella: When Beauty and the Beast Share the Same Mirror

Once we reach a certain stage of life, "image" becomes synonymous with "I'm *aged*!" For me, that stage began the year I received a makeup mirror for Mother's Day. You know, so I could see my chin hairs clearly enough to pluck them. I was actually rather excited about the gift until I plugged it in, lit it up, and flipped it to the Giant Face side. That's when I screamed, "Why didn't you tell me I've been walking around looking like a friggin' hobbit?!"

I had enough hair on my chin (and my upper lip, coming out of my nose, and constructing a furry suspension bridge between my eyebrows) to qualify me as an honorary member of ZZ Top. My fun little freckles had mutated into age spots, giving me the complexion of a speckled hyena. Then there was the 3-D version of the Grand Canyon where my laugh lines used to be. And believe me, I wasn't laughing.

I figured that perhaps what I needed was professional help. Since my daughter's wedding was coming up, I scheduled a makeover. I've never been one to wear much makeup. A touch of blush and a hint of mascara and I'm ready to roll. At least, that's how I rolled before the makeup mirror incident. It was obviously time to bring in the heavy artillery. Spackle, duct tape, magic marker…whatever it took.

The beautician who worked with my daughter on her wedding day was marvelous. Katrina has always been beautiful, even without a hint of makeup. (And I'm not just saying that because I'm her mother! Of course, everyone tells Katrina she looks like her father. 'Nuf said.) But when Katrina was finished, she looked like a storybook princess.

I'm a realist. I knew my beautician couldn't work the same fairy-tale magic on an aging mother-of-the-bride. But I didn't even get close to the storybook realm. When I saw myself in the mirror for the first time, I found a Kabuki dancer staring back at me. I teared up—and not because it was my daughter's wedding day. But I refused to let those tears fall. (Frankly, I was afraid the heavy liner and mascara would run, transforming Kabuki into Pagliacci.) I just kept repeating in my head, "It's not about you. It's about Katrina.

Just suck it up and smile!"

I tried. Then my son Ryan walked by and I couldn't help but whisper, "I look like the guy from *A Clockwork Orange*."

"No, you don't, Mom," Ryan replied. Then he added with a smile, "He only had one eye done."

Yes, as we age, trying hard to retain youthful beauty can prove to be an epic fail. We struggle with more than our weight. We struggle with the whole package.

When we reach biddydom, that age-old question now becomes an old-age question: Am I beautiful? Regardless of how we answered that question when we were young, we're forced to face it again in a whole new light. And hopefully that light has a dimmer switch.

PAPER OR PLASTIC

Fellow biddies, if beauty really is only skin deep, we're in trouble. Because our body is covered with the stuff and, frankly, it's seen better days. If we're moms, we first noticed it start to decline with pregnancy. Stretch marks—our children's very first gift to us—clued us in to the fact that our once stretchy, resilient epidermis has its limits. Cellulite soon added its own unique take on design.

Now, as we move through the perimenopausal years and beyond, age spots, wrinkles, and a loss of collagen and elasticity begin transforming our former porcelain complexion to the consistency of crumpled paper (many sheets of which seem to have either coffee cup stains or connect-the-dots puzzles already printed on them). And it's not just our faces. Like a covert Dr. Frankenstein, someone apparently switched out our hands with some crinkled old lady's while we were sleeping.

Being very fair skinned, I inherited the hands of a ninety-year-old long before I finished my fifties. My skin tears at the slightest scratch, leaving my mitts looking like I've been out dancing with Freddy Krueger. At my last appointment, my dentist was so alarmed at the sight of my hands that he asked if I'd been out working in the garden. "Nope," I assured him. "Just trying on bracelets."

Even if we've slathered ourselves in moisturizer and sunscreen, old age takes its toll. So we try every new antiaging formula advertised on TV. Night creams, neck creams, facial serum, retinol, peptides, bee pollen, BB creams, CC creams…to no avail. A recent study by a marketing research firm found that 56 percent of women who use antiaging products aren't sure they work. But we continue using them anyway.

Hope springs eternal when it comes to a woman's desire to feel beautiful. Even after that woman enters her Biddy Years. But, for some women, hope isn't quite strong enough. They give laser, Botox, or collagen treatments a try. Maybe they even head to a plastic surgeon. Personally, I've never been tempted to go that route, because I'd rather spend my money on travel. When I travel, no one knows who I am, so what I look like is irrelevant. Problem solved.

Besides, we've all seen the results of plastic surgery gone awry. Women whose lips look like castanets and whose eyes are pulled so far back that, to their children's surprise, they really *do* have eyes in the back of their head. These once perfectly lovely looking women now resemble Norma Desmond. And I think we can all agree, no one wants a close-up.

Of course, there is the option of having work done a little farther south, where the results are less obvious to the eye. We can boost up our booty, tuck in our tummies, or suck the fat right out of our thighs. All for a price. For considerably less money, and with a much shorter recovery time, we can purchase shapewear. From control-top panties to a full-on bodysuit, we can hold everything in that wants to hang out without going under the knife. As long as we don't mind holding our breath for hours at a time.

Our final option is to actually lose weight through diet and exercise. Unfortunately, if we're actually successful there's no guarantee our skin will snap right back into shape. It may hang like living room draperies, swaying in a summer breeze.

When it comes to our aging body, we can suck it in with shapewear. We can suck it out with surgery. But the only permanent solution to our quest for biddy beauty is simply to suck it up. Accept our AARP discount with pride, as well as the body, and the skin, that comes along with it. I hear you. It's easier said that done. But God graciously provides help from an unexpected source.

RANDOM ACTS OF BLINDNESS

Grandma Mardel never liked her skin—young or old—because of its color. She was of Portuguese descent and considered the lovely, tawny hues of her complexion substandard to fairer skin tones. So every day she layered on so much white powder, set off by ruby red lips, that she could easily have been mistaken for a descendent of Ronald McDonald instead of the Azore Islands.

Talk about a rut. How we view ourselves is a rut often carved out early in life. If we were teased about our freckles as a kid, we continue to try and conceal them now. If we hated our nose in junior high, our schnoz probably doesn't look any better in our eyes today—unless we've paid to have it surgically enhanced. We're convinced if we can alter, conceal, or eliminate our "flaws," we'll finally have a shot at being beautiful.

That's because we've bought into the lie that beauty is about perfection. Flawless skin. An impossible Barbie-doll figure. Good hair days every day. But it's perception, not perfection, that makes something beautiful. If you're a mom, you undoubtedly saw your newborn as beautiful, even if he had ears the size of satellite dishes. Those we love are beautiful in our eyes and grow even more attractive as the years go by. Perhaps it's time we learned to love ourselves just a little bit more.

This season of life offers us the perfect opportunity to do just that. And it begins with reading glasses.

Just yesterday on social media, a friend posted a funky eye test. It looked like a photo of Albert Einstein—until I took off my readers. Instantly, it morphed into a photo of Marilyn Monroe. This is great news for biddies!

Let's be honest, first thing in the morning many of us may resemble good old Albert … the wild, thinning hair, the hint of a mustache on our upper lip, a generous sprinkling of age spots, Winston Churchill jowls, and droopy eyelids. So why is this good news? Because we've become so nearsighted that when we look in the mirror we can still see Marilyn Monroe! If we allow ourselves to see her, that is.

The entertainment industry has utilized this trick for years. Why do you think the media uses soft-focus lenses on the more mature female newscasters? (Don't get me started on why all the gray-haired male newscasters seem to remain crisply in focus!) God came up with this plan long before the media did. He softens our eyesight as we age. This allows us to more easily overlook so-called imperfections and focus on what's really important: the person inside, the one beneath the skin.

In the Bible's Old Testament, we read about Saul, who failed miserably as king of Israel. In 1 Samuel 16, God put Samuel in charge of anointing a new king, chosen from one of Jesse's sons. When Samuel arrived at Jesse's house, he saw Eliab, the eldest. Apparently, Eliab must have been the George Clooney of the family, because Samuel's first response was, "This has got to be the one!"

But God replied, "Samuel, don't think Eliab is the one just because he's tall and handsome. He isn't the one I've chosen. People judge others by what they look like, but I judge people by what is in their hearts" (1 Samuel 16:7 CEV).

Granted, David wasn't in the room yet. We're told that future king David "was a healthy, good-looking boy with a sparkle in his eyes" (1 Samuel 16:12 CEV). In other Bible translations, he's described as "ruddy," which leads some theologians to believe he was a redhead. My Grandma Kitty would be appalled. She would never believe a man, or a woman, with red hair could be good-looking. But that's human eyes for you. They miss the big picture and give insignificant minutiae center stage.

God wasn't choosing a "younger man" for the job. He was choosing the best man. And it had absolutely nothing to do with the way he looked or the number of years he'd lived. Being an equal opportunity Creator, I believe God feels the same way about women. It's what's beneath our skin that counts.

Almost 2,400 years ago, the Greek philosopher Plato said, "When physical eyesight declines, spiritual eyesight increases." Spiritual eyes look at the world the way God does. They can clearly see that our bodies are not who we are. Our bodies are simply the transportation we move around in.

Whether we're riding in a beat-up VW Bug or a brand-new Lamborghini, it doesn't change who we are. We may prefer one over the other, but either one will get us to our friend's house to cheer her up when she's down. Certainly our friend won't care which ride we came in.

Inside you and me there is loveliness that doesn't need creams or concealer to enhance its good looks. It grows in beauty with every passing year. It's the image of God reflected in us. Not in the mirror, but in our hearts, where His love, grace, compassion, and forgiveness continue to grow.

That doesn't mean a biddy's only beauty is found within. We can still find Marilyn in our mirror if we look with kind eyes. We can also find Einstein if that's who we're more focused on seeing. But unlike us (Albert included), Marilyn never received the gift of growing old. In our mind's eye, her youthful beauty never deepens and matures. It remains static, frozen in time.

In contrast, you and I continue to change and grow, day by day, inside and out. Every new morning is a fresh opportunity to become more comfortable in our very own skin, regardless of what shape that skin is in.

CHAPTER SIX

One Hot Mama— Or One Haute Mess?

You can take the girl out of Berkeley, but you can't take Berkeley out of the girl. Granted, I never actually lived in the city limits of Berkeley, California. But I was born right next door in Oakland and spent the first twelve years of my life living in the East Bay. During those years, fashion went wild, along with everyone under the age of thirty.

On the weekends, my family would drive through the UC Berkeley campus or to San Francisco's Haight Ashbury district to go "hippie watching." The long hair, peasant dresses, love beads, and bell-bottoms made my parents laugh. As for me? I was busy taking fashion tips.

So when we moved one hour north to Santa Rosa in the middle of my seventh-grade year, the outfit I wore for my first day of school wasn't all that surprising: a hot pink psychedelic print minidress with lace insets on the sleeves (handmade by my mother) and white patent leather go-go boots with matching fishnet stockings. I finished it off with my signature accessory, a plastic peace symbol I'd glued onto a strip of leather that I tied around my neck. With my long, stick-straight red hair swinging in the breeze, I felt like the height of fashion. Then the principal opened the classroom door to introduce the "new kid" to her fellow students.

You know that dream about going onstage and suddenly realizing you've forgotten to put on your clothes? Yeah, it felt just like that.

The other girls in the class appeared to have taken vows for some kind of monastic scholastic order. I remember a blur of wool skirts, mostly plaid, many with giant gold safety pins locking the pleats tightly in place. Turtleneck sweaters. Knee-high socks and penny loafers. Headbands, braids, or barrettes kept every lose hair under control.

I never wore that dress again.

At my twentieth high school reunion, someone I'd known since junior high commented, "I can still remember what you wore the first day you walked into class!" Then she began laughing hysterically and headed back to the bar. Talk about lasting impressions.

Take it from me, what we choose to wear matters. That's because clothing can be a form of communication. It sends a message to those around us about who we are—or who we want others to think we are.

We can literally spell out this message—like I do when I wear my sweatshirt that reads: *I like to party and by party I mean read books!*—or our message can be implied by the style, label, or cut of our clothing. For example, at church one Sunday, a female usher leaned over to hand me the offering bag. Nothing out of the ordinary, right? However, her sundress was cut so low and her décolletage was oh so decoratively on display that my first impulse was to place my offering in her cleavage. You'll be relieved to know I refrained.

In this woman's defense, I don't believe she intended to send the message I received so clearly that morning. After all, we live in Phoenix, land of perpetual summer. Having one hundred days a year where temperatures soar over one hundred degrees does seem to encourage a garden of Eden approach to fashion: naked and not ashamed. But, like hitting that "send" button before taking time to carefully evaluate what's written in an e-mail, this woman's message was out there. Mistakes and all.

We can laugh off what we choose to put on. We can say God doesn't really care about anything as trivial as our clothes, so neither should we. But consider how picky God was about the attire of the priests in the Old Testament. In Exodus 28, we read about robes, sashes, turbans, and breastplates embellished with precious stones, embroidered pomegranates, and gold bells. God dictated exactly what Aaron and his sons put on, right down to their linen underwear.

This priestly clothing was exquisitely beautiful, but it also told a story. Each piece communicated a symbolic message about God and His people. Exodus 28:40 tells us that what the priests wore gave them "dignity and honor" (NIV). The Hebrew word for *dignity* can also mean "beauty." As part of this ongoing "royal priesthood" (1 Peter 2:9 NIV), should you and I dress to express anything less?

INSIDE I'M STILL WEARING A BIKINI

So God has a sense of style. So did we. Then we hit the Biddy Years. Time to trade in our stilettos for sensible shoes and our daisy dukes for elastic-waist potluck pants. Or is it?

Just like the Old Testament priests, we used to have hard-and-fast rules about fashion: be sure your shoes, belt, and bag match; don't wear white after Labor Day; shun miniskirts, bikinis, and long hair after the age of forty; don't wear two prints at the same time, etc.

One fashion rule I grew up hearing over and over again was that redheads should never wear red. However, when my mother took me shopping for school clothes each year, she let me pick out one outfit all on my own. You can guess what I chose. A red plaid ruffled dress became one of my personal elementary school favorites. Admittedly, I've always been a bit of a fashion rebel. Thank you, Berkeley.

Today, I still feel like the same girl I was back in those flower power days. On the inside, at least. So now that every fashion rule I've ever heard has been turned on its head and my mother no longer mandates what hangs in my closet, there's a temptation to purchase all of the outfits I didn't get to wear when I was young—or to wear the same styles that worked for me back then. The ones that made me feel pretty or skinny or sexy or strong. But trust me: no one wants to see this gray-haired matron in a red plaid ruffled dress or patent leather go-go boots.

That revelation came to me at a Rolling Stones concert. I was in my late thirties and awestruck at how old rocker Jagger (a mere fifty-one at the time) could still sprint, strut, and swagger across the stage song after song. But it was the action offstage that really grabbed my attention. I'd never seen a gathering of so many menopausal women sporting skin-tight black leather pants in my entire life. Let me assure you, it wasn't pretty. I swore I'd never make the same mistake.

Fast-forward twenty years. One night as I was sorting photographs, I came across a picture of my mother—and she was wearing *my* clothes. I did a double take. Yup, my "mother" was me. At least she wasn't wearing skin-tight leather pants. But I saw myself as others undoubtedly do. And that mental picture stays with me when I shop.

At one time in our lives, we may have been hip and hot. Now we lean more toward big hips and hot flashes. So we'd better learn to dress the part. That doesn't mean we have to dye our hair blue and stock up on muumuus and support hose. But it does mean that perhaps we should retire that string bikini—or at least repurpose it to tie up a rib roast.

Oliver Wendell Holmes said, "The young know the rules. The old know the exceptions." My general rule when it comes to clothing is if my daughter would wear it, it's probably too young. But if my mother would wear it, it's probably too old. But, as Mr. Holmes would attest, there are always exceptions.

God created us as individuals, each with our own unique personality—and distinctive fashion sense to match. I have friends whose favorite colors are khaki, white, and navy. Others can pull off a hat worthy of the Kentucky Derby while dining at Kentucky Fried Chicken. Some are consistently decked out in the latest couture, and some only shop at secondhand stores. As for me? I think my daughter-in-law summed it up best when she peeked in my closet and remarked, "You're obviously a woman who's not afraid of prints!"

Two fashion accessories I treasure are a string of faux pearls and a pair of genuine mink poodle pins with rhinestone eyes. Not that I ever wear either. But each is a treasured keepsake from one of my grandmothers. It doesn't take Coco Chanel to guess who wore what. Depending on my mood, I can follow in the fashion footsteps of either one. I can go full Mardel and wear a leopard-print sweater with oversized, blingy earrings. Or I can set my inner Kitty free and don a classic navy cardigan that would pair perfectly with a set of pearls. Though I'd personally be more likely to pair it with my Union Jack–print TOMS.

Though each one of us has her own signature style, there are many different women inside us all. Women whose choice of clothes communicate a message about who we are, how we feel about ourselves, and how we fit (or don't fit) in with those around us on this particular day. So, what message are you currently clothed in?

HIDE OR SEEK … OR CHIC?

Back when we were younger, our "message" wasn't underwritten by the labels on our clothes but by the labels we attached to ourselves. Pretty. Plain. Creative. Sexy. Smart. Insignificant. Skinny. Curvy. Big-boned. Funny. Shy. Outgoing. Insignificant. Tough. Wounded. Beautiful. We tried these descriptors on like we do jeans at the mall. Some we discarded as ill fitting. Others we've clung to for years. Some we wear only because someone else told us we should.

Though the outside picture we present to the world is a complex ensemble of personality, self-image, and style, its main message generally falls into one of two categories: hide or seek. In other words, "Don't notice me" or "Please notice me."

Those who long to hide in plain sight may wear oversized clothing to conceal their true shape. Some shun prints and bright colors. Others closely follow fashion trends, but it's because they're afraid to draw negative attention to themselves by breaking the rules. There are even those who try to hide by choosing in-your-face message tees or outfits that border on costumes. While they appear to be seeking attention, what they really want is for people to focus on their outlandish getup (as both my grandmothers used to say)—and not on the person wearing them.

What's interesting is the ultimate goal of the "seek" crowd is often exactly the same. They dress to impress (and often to excess!), because they equate so much of their personal worth with how they look instead of who they are. When those accustomed to seeking (and receiving) attention through their appearance enter the Biddy Years, they can easily slip into the "mutton dressed up as lamb" syndrome. Squeezing ourselves into clothing that is too tight, too revealing, or simply "too" everything is just begging for a wardrobe malfunction. Besides, a menopausal woman who wears "Juicy" on the back end and "Spoiled" on the front is simply inviting a comparison with rotting fruit.

Speaking of fruit, let's head back to the garden of Eden for a moment. Remember why Adam and Eve donned those fig leaves? They were ashamed. They were trying to hide. Sound familiar?

Neither "hide" nor "seek" is a way of dressing with dignity and honor. Instead of dressing to cover up who we are, let's dress to express who God created us to be. Ephesians 2:10 tells us, "We are God's masterpiece. He has created us anew in Christ Jesus, so we can do the good things he planned for us long ago" (NLT). Let's dress in what's appropriate for the job at hand.

Want a few pointers on what that might be? Take a tip from a recent study done at the University of Hertfordshire in England.[1] Researchers tested a group of students, some wearing Superman shirts and others wearing their own clothing. Those wearing the Man of Steel apparel consistently proved physically stronger and mentally superior to those who did not. Apparently what we wear can influence how we see ourselves—and vice versa.

What's the Superman tee in your closet? Do you feel confident and capable whenever you wear those red heels? Do your favorite jeans make you feel authentic and approachable, ready to do whatever needs to be done? Forget what others think. Concentrate on the day ahead. What "good things" do you believe God has planned for you today?

Instead of trying to hide, show up. Allow your true self to be seen, clothed with dignity and honor. Choose to dress for God's best—that includes living out your life as the original, remarkable, uniquely fashionable woman He designed you to be.

---

1 *Oprah* magazine, January 2015, 88.

CHAPTER SEVEN

Paging Dr. Pepper...

My name is Vicki and I'm an addict. My habit began shortly after birth. My first word was *Mama*. My second was *Twirt*. For the uninitiated, that's baby talk for Squirt, a sugary, carbonated grapefruit soda. From the first day my parents put this elixir of the gods in my baby bottle, I was hooked. Considering how young I was when my habit began, it's surprising I have a cavity-free tooth left in my head.

By elementary school, I'd graduated to the hard stuff. Namely Dr. Pepper. It had sugar, bubbles, and the added benefit of caffeine. It also had twenty-three secret ingredients, rumored to be exotic things like coriander, anise, allspice, ginger, amaretto, and plum—the latter of which we all know is just a prune that's still wearing a training bra. Today, Dr. Pepper remains my prune juice of choice.

But I want to assure you I can quit at any time. During both of my pregnancies, I did not imbibe a single drop. (In honor of full disclosure, this was before Dr. Pepper was available caffeine free.) I'm not proud of my tiny little dependency problem, but I've never hidden it. After all, I've heard that secrecy can be a sign of a *real* addiction.

Everyone who knows me well knows about my fizzy little indiscretion. One friend even gave me a sign that reads, "I'm ugly without my Dr. Pepper." Of course, I can be ugly with it as well. Like the time my husband and I got into an ever-so-slightly heated argument in the car and I dumped my ice-cold can of the Doctor right on his, uh … man parts. To be fair, I lay the blame for that incident squarely on being menopausal, not over-caffeinated. And just an eensy-teensy little bit on Mark for not seeing things my way.

Honestly, I rarely use Dr. Pepper as a weapon. But I do lean on it as a muse. Since I've never been a coffee drinker, the Doctor helps push my slow-moving brain into gear so I can create a cohesive sentence. Or dress myself in clothes that match. Albeit, I now drink the diet version since my metabolism moves even more slowly than my thought processes.

So should I worry? Is Dr. Pepper a simple pleasure or a carbonated crutch? Are ruts like these helpful or harmful, especially as we enter the Biddy Years? If we're honest, we all have our proclivities—which is a fancy way of saying we have weaknesses we choose to indulge. How can we tell when these indulgences go too far?

THE NOT-SO-GREAT ESCAPE

Lights, action, silver dollars … Put Grandma Mardel in a casino and she not only played 21, she acted like it was the age on her driver's license. She'd wrestle multiple one-armed bandits at a time, go without eating all day, and move faster across the casino floor than a showgirl at quitting time. But on one trip when Mardel was in her nineties, I watched her rosy-cheeked excitement suddenly morph to pallid gray. In what seemed like slow motion, she slid off her slot-machine stool right onto the casino carpet. At that exact same moment, bells starting ringing, lights started flashing, and silver dollars started pouring out of her machine with that "ka-chunk, ka-chunk, ka-chunk" sound that makes gamblers' adrenaline spike an all-time high.

My first thought was, "This is exactly how Grandma would want to meet her Maker—on a winning streak!"

As I pondered the possibility that perhaps every time a bell rings an angel really *does* get her wings, the paramedics arrived. Mardel slowly sat up, blinked her eyes a time or two, brushed aside my helping hand, and began hurriedly scooping her winnings into her bucket. One of the paramedics slowed her down long enough to check her pulse and inquire, "So, ma'am, what happened?"

"Well," she began, her rosy-cheeked excitement quickly returning, "first I was playing the slots at Bronco Billy's, but I wasn't winning anything, so I headed down here to the Brass Ass and started playing the dollar slots over in that corner over there, but I could tell they just weren't with me today, so I headed over here to the slots, and even though it took a while, I started winning…"

Here was my grandmother, a borderline hypochondriac, speaking to someone working in the medical field, and all she could talk about was how Lady Luck was treating her that day. I knew she was going to be just fine.

So was my grandmother's gambling "just fine"? Or should it have been cause for concern? Gambling used to be considered the devil's playground. These days, churchgoers are more likely to put it in the same category as appletinis. So acceptable, they're almost passé. Many churches even sponsor events that feature forms of gambling, like Bunco, bingo, fantasy football, and raffle tickets. The general consensus is that if we've got disposable income and are simply playing a game, there's nothing inherently wrong with spending money on amusement.

When amusement and pleasure go underground, that's when I believe they cross the line into enslavement. It's all about the secrets we keep. Those little habits we'd be embarrassed for folks at church to find out about. The shopping bags from the mall we hide from our husband. The bowl (or carton) of ice cream we eat after everyone else has gone to bed. The sites on the Internet we'd quickly ⸻ ᵏ off if anyone else entered the room.

The Internet alone has opened so many new rabbit hole for us biddies to fall into if we so choose. We can gamble, shop, view pornography, or stalk an old beau from high school on Facebook all in the privacy (and secrecy) of our own home. As we enter the Biddy Years, we have more free time, more time by ourselves, and often more disposable income. Each one of these gives us more opportunities to do whatever we want—for better or for worse. And to do it without anyone else becoming the wiser.

In 1 Corinthians 6:12, Paul writes, "You say, 'I am allowed to do anything'—but not everything is good for you. And even though 'I am allowed to do anything,' I must not become a slave to anything" (NLT).

Have we become slaves? In other words, is there anything we consistently turn to instead of God when we're stressed, depressed, or simply want to escape our humdrum biddy life? This question is worth careful consideration because some destructive habits we simply slide into without paying much attention. Before we know it, we're stuck in a rut that's leading us down a road we never intended to travel. The longer we stay there, the deeper the rut and the harder it is to turn around.

OF MICE AND MENOPAUSE

Let's talk rodents. Not fictional ones like Mickey and Minnie, Chuck E. Cheese, or Stuart Little. We're talking unnamed heroes—the unwitting subjects in the research lab. Back in the late 1970s, a Canadian psychologist named Bruce Alexander headed up a project that became known as Rat Park. At the time, experiments relating to drug addiction were big news. They all seemed to prove that if these tiny test subjects (whose responses are similar to us much larger humans) were given access to opiates, such as heroine or morphine, they'd consistently choose to dope themselves. Sometimes to the point of death.

But Alexander noted one constant in these experiments: all of the rodents were isolated in separate cages. Rats are smart, social critters. Like us. Maybe the caged rats were lonely, depressed, and unhappy to begin with. I know I would be if I were locked in a cage without a good book, Netflix, or an occasional girls' night out.

So Alexander constructed a rodent resort. Rat Park was two hundred times the size of standard research cages. Instead of metal bars, it had decorated walls, running wheels, and cozy nesting areas filled with clean wood chips. Best of all, the whole rat pack, guys and gals, got to hang out together.

Along with plenty of food, the rodents had a supply of fresh water and sugar water laced with morphine (sugar helps hide the drug's bitter taste).

The results? Rat Park rodents chose plain water twenty times more frequently than their caged peers. Furthermore, when a drug that blocked the effects of morphine was added to the sugar water, consumption actually went up a bit.[1] Proving that rats, like me, sometimes just want a little sugar water to sweeten their day.

Like the residents of Rat Park, the better we feel about ourselves and our surroundings, the more likely we'll be to make balanced, healthy choices instead of becoming dependent on a not-so-great escape. This doesn't mean we should run out and buy a bigger house or force our decor into furniture rehab. We don't need to build our own Rat Park. We need to break free of whatever cage we've built around ourselves.

The bars of our own individual cage are forged from personal battles with things like loneliness, bitterness, disillusionment, fear, perfectionism, or a lack of self-esteem. The key to unlocking our cage isn't more willpower. It's a change of heart. That begins by taking an honest look at the heart of our problem.

You've heard of the FICO score, which measures the strength of your credit. Let's talk about our pica score. Never heard of it? That's because I just made it up. But whenever I think about addiction of any kind, I think about pica—which is an eating disorder where people crave things that hold absolutely no nutritional value, like dirt, clay, rocks … and, I guess, Diet Dr. Pepper. Sometimes pica is caused by anemia. Our bodies are craving iron, but we try to fix that by feeding them stones.

---

1   Tom Stafford, "Drug Addiction: The Complex Truth," *BBC Future* article, September 10, 2013, http://www.bbc.com/future/story/20130910-drug-addiction-the-complex-truth.

Matthew 7:9 asks, "Which of you, if your son asks for bread, will give him a stone?" (NIV). We will, in a sense. Our very own bodies are crying out for necessities like love, comfort, rest, encouragement, community, or time with God. Instead, we feed them trips to the mall, romance novels, online gambling, cupcakes, and binge watching old episodes of *The X-Files*.

Having officially reached the Biddy Years, you'd think we'd know better by now. We're no longer naive, emotional teens. We're supposed to be older and wiser. But we're also facing a season of change—The Change, to be exact. Change fuels feelings of chaos and a loss of control. That's the kind of emotional environment ripe for breeding new addictions and dependencies.

Did you know that 13 percent of women over the age of fifty exhibit symptoms of eating disorders?[2] It's not just an adolescent problem. Menopausal weight gain is only one source of the current chaos in our lives that we try to gain control over. If we do lose weight, we get such positive reinforcement from those around us that there's little incentive to stop.

Of course, the other 87 percent of us may feel we can overlook our little biddy proclivities because they aren't as potentially deadly as an eating disorder. But that doesn't mean they aren't killing us on the inside. If we're serious

---

2 Michelle Konstantinovsky, "Not Your Daughter's Eating Disorder," *Oprah* magazine, May 2013.

about choosing life, we need to stage an intervention—for ourselves. Let's be honest about the cages we've built in our lives and the drug(s) of choice we're mainlining to deal with them.

In treatment centers and twelve-step programs, those struggling to climb out of a destructive rut are paired with a sponsor. Asking a friend to hold us accountable for a positive change we want to make in our lives is helpful. But it's also helpful to become our own sponsor. That means treating ourselves kindly, with compassion and grace. It's encouraging ourselves to do what's best for us in the long run, not what may feel good in the moment. It's praying for insight into the "whys" behind our cages and the "hows" of filling our emotional hunger with nourishment that will actually satisfy.

In the words of the fourteenth-century Persian poet Hafez:

Run my dear,
From anything
That may not strengthen
Your precious budding wings.

We may not run as fast as we used to. But every choice we make is a step forward or a step back. If we're already headed downhill, it only makes sense to keep moving ahead!

CHAPTER EIGHT

All the Wrong Stuff

You're aware of my soda addiction. So it should come as no surprise that when visiting my folks' house, I would scour their fridge for a bubbly little pick-me-up while awaiting their return from work. That's when I spied it, hidden in the back behind a wall of take-out boxes, plastic containers crammed with leftovers, and nearly empty bottles of salad dressing and condiments: a Schweppes Bitter Lemon. Score!

When I was a college student in Italy, a can of soda was more expensive than a glass of wine. So I temporarily switched my allegiance from Dr. Pepper to Schweppes, which was both affordable and readily available. Not a big seller in the States, it had been years since I'd had one. I felt like a gourmand who'd discovered a rare truffle.

I twisted off the cap and took a big swig right out of the

bottle. I gagged. "Funny," I thought, "I don't remember it being … chunky." That's when I looked at the bottle cap in my hand. Printed inside it said, "You may be a winner! Call the number below by Dec. 31, 1983 to receive your free gift." It was 1998. If I'd only known, I wouldn't have opened that bottle. I could've made a killing on *Antiques Roadshow*.

Everyone's fridge needs purging now and then. But at least food warns us when it's time to give it the old heave-ho. It gets squishy. It grows mold. It smells funny. Some of it even has an expiration date printed right on the package. If only the rest of our household goods were so accommodating.

I'll be the first to admit, I wasn't born with the organizational gene. Whatever I own (other than what's balanced precariously in the fridge) will undoubtedly spend some time on the floor, a countertop, or shoved into a junk drawer before it finds its final resting place. Which could be the top of my desk. My office looks like a public library and adjacent paper factory exploded. Then a laptop happened to float gently down and land atop the rubble.

Perhaps you're the exact opposite. Perhaps you ogle the Container Store like I do cupcakes in a bakery case. Maybe you'd give Mr. Clean a run for his money in a "clean enough to eat off my floors" contest. But even if your cotton swabs are lined up in your bathroom drawer like storm troopers standing at attention, it doesn't mean you're immune from stockpiling stuff. It simply means your consumption is a bit less conspicuous than mine.

As a country, we've got a major stuff problem. Can you imagine trying to explain to someone who lives in a third-world country the necessity of a storage unit? Even though the average American home provides three thousand square feet of space, more than 10 percent of us need to rent extra storage to handle the overflow.[1]

But this desire to acquire isn't reserved for homeowners. Even homeless people load up their shopping carts with stuff they happen to find. It may be considered trash, and they may have no use for it, but picking it up and holding onto it provides a kind of comfort. Sounds a lot like the last chapter on addiction, doesn't it? That's because acquiring new stuff, or somebody's old stuff that is new to us, gives our biddy brains that little burst of dopamine. That's the same chemical that other addictive behaviors reward our brain with that makes us feel good. For a while. Then, like Oliver Twist, it pleads, "Please sir (or ma'am), can I have some more?"

Even if family members haven't yet nominated us for an episode of *Hoarders*, most of us surround ourselves with stuff we don't need and, quite possibly, don't even want. Or maybe we do. Maybe the UPS guy knows us by

---

1 Jennifer Calonia, "Why Paying for a Storage Unit is Always a Terrible Idea," August 3, 2014, http://www.gobankingrates.com/savings-account/why-still -wasting-money-storage-units/.

name. Maybe we've filled the kids' old bedrooms with commemorative teacups and antique garden gnomes. Because Scripture isn't totally clear on the topic of whether heaven has storage units, someone, someday is going to have to get rid of all this stuff. It might as well be us. And considering our ever-advancing age, the time might as well be now.

LET'S NOT PUT THE ERR IN HEIRLOOM

Guys have their garages. The more tools they have, the more manly they feel. For those of us who are of the female persuasion, we have our closets. For most women, the more shoes we have … well, the less likely it is we'll actually wear every pair. But the happier we feel! Right? If you're anything like me, it's not just shoes that flow from your closet like soft-serve ice cream. There's also clothing. Lots of clothing.

But in my mind, every closet pales in comparison to Grandma Mardel's. Hers was a bona fide treasure trove. Back when I was a mere youngster, my sister and I played dress up for hours in that cramped, mothball-scented corridor. Mardel's home was built long before walk-in closets were the rage. But Mardel had so much stuff that even if she had a walk-in, chances are she wouldn't have been able to just walk in. She'd have had to push her way through, kind of like riding the subway at rush hour in Tokyo.

Inside her closet there was plenty of everyday stuff, like polyester print dresses and pantsuits. But to the far left, you could actually step back in time. There were gowns and cocktail dresses from the 1920s, thirties, forties, and fifties. They made a sherbet-colored rainbow of taffeta, tulle, satin, and organza. Beaded bodices, sequined skirts, elbow-length gloves, mink stoles, dainty-toed heels, and clutch purses to match. My favorite gown was fit for a prima ballerina. Its sepia-toned underskirt was covered in a billowy net of sea-foam green. Every time I put it on, I felt like Hans Christian Andersen's little mermaid. After her tail transformed into legs, of course.

If only I had those beautiful dresses now. Do you know what I'd do with them? Truth is, I'd probably stuff them in my closet and not do anything with them until it was time to move. Then I'd carefully box them up and transport them to my new address. Someday I'd pass them down to my daughter. Who would shove them in her closet until it was time to move. You get the idea.

Just because something is old doesn't make it an heirloom. The items we treasure are not all worth passing down to our kids. But that's what happens if we refuse to let go. Often, what we're actually handing down is the responsibility to get rid of stuff that's passed its expiration date long ago.

During the Biddy Years, by continuing to accumulate more instead of paring down, we're setting up our next of kin as garbage collectors. What's more, they'll be forced to take on this job during the stressful time of making final arrangements for us. If we want to lessen their grief, I guess this is one way to do it. Resentment is bound to temper their mourning, at least a tad.

So why do we hold on so tightly? Our stuff tells a story. It's our history written in possessions. There's the ribbon we got in second grade for perfect attendance. The deflated balloon from our wedding reception. The baby tooth of our youngest child. The dried head of a piranha we caught fishing on the Amazon River. (Don't laugh. That's one of my personal treasures I just can't seem to let go of.)

Even the clothes in our closet hold cherished memories. There are the pants that used to fit. The dress we wore to our daughter's wedding. The sweater we loved until it got that funny little hole in the front. The outfit that made us feel pretty or skinny or young. The heels that looked so amazing in the store window but then did things to our feet that could have qualified as God's eleventh plague on Egypt.

We need to face the fact that the proverbial glass slippers in our closet do not have the power to magically transform us into the princess we used to be. Especially if those slippers have a hole in the toe. Stuff is just stuff. At this point in our lives, a lot of what we own is like an old boyfriend who isn't interested in us anymore. Let's face it. It's time to let go and move on.

GET YOUR MIND OUT OF THE CLUTTER!

The main thing most women our age want to downsize is our jeans. However, moving to a smaller home is beneficial for many reasons. One, it forces us to ask hard questions. Like, "Whatever possessed me to start collecting beanie babies?" Two, there's nothing like moving to make you want to take a monastic vow of poverty. When you have to pack all your stuff, you're reminded of just how much you own—and how much of it's still in the same cardboard box you moved a decade ago.

I just downsized this month. My home, not my jeans. I got rid of a truckload of stuff. Now that I'm settling into my new little place, what do I want to do? Buy stuff. You know, for the new digs. Stuff that makes it feel like "home."

Home truly is "where the heart is." But all too often, my heart's at the mall. I don't even have to drive there. While writing this chapter, a new email popped up. Thinking it might be work related, I took a moment to check it out. Instead, it alerted me to a blowout sale at a furniture website. I clicked the link. Just to give my mind a quick break, of course. You'll be happy to know I didn't purchase anything. This time. But here I am shopping in my mind for more even while I'm writing about owning less. This, my friends, is not a good sign.

Luke 12:15 tells us, "Be alert and guard your heart from greed and always wishing for what you don't have. For your life can never be measured by the amount of things you possess" (TPT).

The wealth—or poverty—of our inner life is often reflected by our outer life. Is my house cluttered with eternally insignificant stuff? Chances are my heart and mind are as well. Is my closet a time machine, keeping my well-clad foot stuck in the past? No wonder I struggle to accept the aging state of my biddy body. If I'm truly content with God giving me "this day my daily bread," why does my pantry look like I'm squirreling away supplies to provide for the whole community should we come under an extraterrestrial attack?

Contentment isn't found when our house is finally decorated the way we want or when our closet can't hold even one more pair of pumps. It's when we can chime in with Paul and say, "I know what it is to be in need, and I know what it is to have plenty. I have learned the secret of being content in any and every situation, whether well fed or hungry, whether living in plenty or in want" (Philippians 4:12 NIV). That perspective on life germinates from the inside out, not the other way around.

Take it from my grandmothers. Mardel's closet reflected her home. Her two-story house, complete with basement, was stuffed to the brim with everything from porcelain figurines to taxidermied deer heads. To the day she died, she never stopped chasing the dream of winning a lottery-sized jackpot. Grandma Kitty, on the other hand, lived in a small apartment and slept on a Murphy bed that pulled down from the living room wall. When she made the move to assisted living, she was delighted with her new studio apartment and told me, "There's plenty of room here for everything I need."

Enjoying our Biddy Years to the fullest isn't synonymous with cramming them full of stuff. So let's take an honest look at what we have, as well as what we think we need. We don't have to be spring chickens to do some major spring-cleaning any time of year.

By choosing to travel light into the season ahead, we'll spend less time taking care of stuff. This means more time for everything else we want to do and see and everyone we want to lavish a little love on. Besides, the less cluttered our home is, the more easily we'll be able to find where we last set down the keys to our car.

CHAPTER NINE

Out of the Mouths of Babes... Who Happen to be Wearing Depends

M y new friend was hanging out the car window, yelling, "Woohoo!" at the top of her lungs. Nope, we weren't teens drag racing down Main Street. We were two biddies on a road trip. Pam was forty-five and I was pushing the big 5-0. That made the sight of Pam's abandon all the more spectacular.

But what truly won my heart was what she'd confided earlier. "I don't cry often. So my prayer for this trip is that God moves me to the point of tears over something good." This moment was that "something."

Our road trip to Santa Fe was a Getting To Know You

tour, because when it comes to friendship I side with Mark Twain, who wrote, "I have found out that there ain't no surer way to find out whether you like people or hate them than to travel with them." Time to put my friendship with Pam to the test.

We'd only known each other a matter of months, but now we had a nine-hour drive each way to share our life stories. In addition, we had two glorious days to wander Santa Fe's galleries, feast on amazing Mexican food, and chat about anything and everything back at our shared room at the bed-and-breakfast. In other words, lots of together time. By the end of a friendship test like that, you either bond or you bolt. So far, we were fusing like Gorilla Glue®.

When it came time to head home, my VW Bug was apparently none too pleased with the prospect. It refused to roll the passenger side window back up, no matter how sweetly I spoke to the little electric button. But not even traveling 65 mph in below-freezing temps could put a damper on our trip. We donned our jackets, turned on the heated seats, and talked really loudly as we cruised down the highway. We figured we'd better enjoy the cold now, since one-hundred-plus degree temps awaited us when we neared Phoenix.

About an hour into our drive, the incessant whine of the wind and our nearly frostbitten fingers were forgotten. Our attention was focused on the early morning sky, jam-packed with color and craziness. An airborne scarecrow, a gargantuan squirrel, and a barn big enough to hold an ark full of animals floated overhead. Thanks to happenstance and God's great timing, we'd landed smack dab in the middle of the Albuquerque International Balloon Fiesta, the largest ballooning event in the world. More than seven hundred hot air balloons provided quintessential sunrise entertainment.

That's when Pam had her "woohoo" moment, accompanied by frantic photo snapping out the permanently open window. And yup, those photos were taken through tears. As for me, that was the moment I knew Pam was a friend worth holding onto.

A decade has passed since that road trip. Today I continue to count Pam as one of my closest friends. Not to say she doesn't have her faults. She continues to look so young that not once, but twice, people have mistaken me for her mother. (Okay, so one of those people was a guy in Las Vegas walking up a down escalator with a very large drink in his hand. But the other person seemed perfectly sober.) Not only that, Pam wears a size 000 at Chico's. Seriously, 000 isn't a size. It's antimatter.

It takes a lot for a biddy to overlook a friend who continues to appear youthful *and* thin in the face of aging. But Pam's worth it. She never makes me feel old or overweight (although some days I can choose to feel that way all on my own!). From where I stand today, Pam appears to be a biddy buddy for life.

But as we move forward and "old friend" becomes literal, do our relationships change? You bet your sweet biddy they do. What that change looks like will depend on the ruts we allow ourselves to slide into.

ALL BY MY SELFIE

As biddies, friendship looks a bit different than it did in our teens. Instead of sharing pictures of boyfriends or heart-throbs from *Tiger Beat* magazine, we trade snapshots of our grandchildren or our latest bone density scan. Instead of sharing each other's clothes, we share reading glasses, so our friend can see clearly enough inside her purse to locate her own pair. Now slumber parties happen spontaneously. All we have to do is turn on a movie we actually want to see, and one of us will be snoring and drooling in no time. We're also more ecstatic about sharing that we have a clean colon than having clear skin.

Also, once upon a time, befriending kindred spirits was accomplished by spending time with them—in person. Today, we not only befriend, but defriend. And it can all be done with the click of a button. Online we can be "friends" with people we've never met and never plan on meeting. Why say yes to their request? Because when people "like" our status or our latest selfie, we mistakenly believe they're "liking" us. The more likes we get, the better we feel about ourselves. For the moment. Or until our next post doesn't get the clicks we believe it deserves. Then, we suddenly morph into that kid picked last on the dodgeball team, whose inner voice strikes up a chorus of, "Nobody likes me, everybody hates me. I'm gonna eat some worms!"

If we're honest with ourselves, we know this has nothing to do with friendship. It's more akin to digital narcissism. How many followers we have on social media does not reflect the true size of our circle of friends. No one can really be friends with 547 individuals. At least not friends who are actively involved in each other's lives.

A real relationship isn't built by viewing pics of someone's egg salad sandwich or their cat dressed as Queen Nefertiti. We don't need more people we can poke or wink or send smiley faces to online. We need friends who can hug us with honest-to-goodness arms when we need it. Even if those arms jiggle as they console.

Real friendship takes time. More time than a single click of a mouse. As biddies, that's something we've got. Our schedules are often freer and more flexible than they've been in years. But when it comes to spending time with friends, all too often a short text or email replaces what once would have been an actual conversation or phone call. We play Words With Friends® instead of actually speaking to our friends. An e-card or Facebook message is swapped out for the birthday cards and letters we used to sign with our very own hand. Today's preferred forms of communication are all just so efficient. And so much less personal.

What's more worrisome is that many of us are choosing

to spend our extra free time with a big-screen TV instead of with actual people. I understand the appeal. When we connect with a television character or a "real" person on a reality show, we feel like we get to know them. They make us laugh. They make us cry. We care about what happens to them. That feels like friendship.

News flash: it isn't reciprocal. But it is comfortable. Being a sofa spud doesn't take any energy, effort, or social graces. We can hang out with the "cool kids" like Ross and Rachel or Mad Men or James Bond without running the risk of rejection. We can turn them off if they make us mad or binge watch them if we're feeling lonely. We're in control. Unlike in actual relationships.

But all of these baby steps we're taking toward virtual friendship, in place of an honest-to-goodness roller coaster ride of real relationship, is quietly misleading us into a rut of isolation. If we don't actively nurture the friendships we have, as well as continue adding new friends along the way, we may find ourselves spending our latter biddy years flying solo.

Did you know that loneliness can increase a person's mortality risk by 45 percent? To help put that in perspective, obesity increases our risk by 23 percent and excessive alcohol use by 37 percent. Lonely elderly people are also 64 percent more likely to develop dementia than those with a strong circle of friends.[1]

Yet again, the choice is ours: life or death, blessings or

1   Sanjay Gupta, MD, "Just Say Hello," *Oprah* magazine, March 2014, 125.

curses, love or loneliness. Jesus told His disciples, "A new commandment I give to you, that you love one another; as I have loved you" (John 13:34 NKJV). How can we love one another if we choose to spend all our time alone? Clicking "like" on Facebook doesn't count.

Okay, enough of the Debbie Downer rant. But this is life-changing stuff. We're never too old to welcome new friends into our lives or to reconnect on a deeper level with those friends we already have. Yes, it takes time and effort. It even involves risk. Rejection, careless words, and hurt feelings don't just happen in grade school. But if Jesus was willing to give His life so we could be wholehearted friends with God, can't we at least be willing to pick up the phone and invite a fellow biddy to lunch?

OLD FRIENDS ARE THE BEST MEDICINE

So I've filled your little gray head with the hazards of sliding into a rut of loneliness. Now it's time to celebrate the blessings of having a strong, supportive circle of friends. Just a few of its proven benefits include: lower stress, fewer colds, better sleep, lower blood pressure, and a sharper memory, as well as that whole longevity thing.[2] Not to mention that friendship is flat-out fun!

From grade school to the present day, I've enjoyed the privilege of being part of an amazing, ever-changing circle of friends. But back when I lived in Colorado Springs, when

2 Ibid.

I was still a relatively young whippersnapper of a woman, I was still the oldest person in every group I hung out with. I repeatedly asked God to bring an older woman into my life, a friend and mentor who'd "been there, done that" and lived to tell the tale. So God moved me to Phoenix, land of retirees and snowbirds. To my delight, I now have a potential smorgasbord of geriatric pals.

Today my circle of friends includes women in their twenties, thirties, forties, fifties, sixties, seventies, and eighties. Each one adds her own unique gift of love and laughter to my life. But it's the older women whose advice I cherish most. Their words of wisdom aren't conjecture. They've already walked the roads I need the most help navigating right now.

Proverbs 13:20 says, "If you want to grow in wisdom, then spend time with the wise. Walk with the wicked and you'll eventually become just like them" (TPT). This means I not only need to choose friendship over isolation but also carefully choose who I include in my inner circle of friends, regardless of their age and mine.

When it comes to acquaintances, my circle is wide. I like to hang out with folks from every walk of life. I don't care if their lifestyle, spiritual beliefs, or mother tongue doesn't jive with my own. I have a lot to learn about what it's like to walk in their shoes. I enjoy spending time with them, talking with them, asking them lots of questions. They expand my understanding of what love looks like.

But when it comes to my closest confidants, the friends

with whom I share most of my time and my heart, I choose women I'd like to grow up to be. Women I admire. Women whose advice I can trust. Women who remind me a lot of Jesus.

That's the kind of biddy, and friend, I want to be. I may be a younger woman to my friends in their seventies, but I'm currently stepping into the orthopedic oxfords of an older woman and mentor to those for whom menopause isn't yet a blip on their hormonal radar. When they turn to me for advice, I want to make certain I help guide them down the road God would most want them to travel.

Neither of my grandmothers had a close circle of friends. Grandma Kitty's jealous husband cut her off from having much of a social life during their marriage. After he died, Kitty was so shy that other than writing letters to a couple of friends she'd made early in life, she spent most of her days sitting on the sidelines of friendship. Such a loss. I still consider her one of the sweetest friends I've ever had. She certainly filled a mentor role for me.

As for Grandma Mardel, she didn't have much use for people who didn't share her bloodline. Family was paramount. We were expected to meet her every need, both physical and emotional. She did have a social circle, though you couldn't really call it a circle of friends. Mardel appeared to pave her relational way with gifts and cash, not out of generosity, but as insurance that people would come back for more.

When Mardel wasn't bribing her acquaintances, she was trying to impress them. She wanted others to know she had the fanciest car, the ritziest party dress, and the most devoted husband. She wanted others to recognize how important she was. Unfortunately, I don't think Mardel believed her own press.

In my opinion, what lay at the heart of both of my grandmothers' lack of friends was the fact that they never personally believed they were worthy of other people's time. They never felt they were "enough" by simply being the women God created them to be.

When it comes to friendship, we need to be the kind of friend we're looking for in others. To do that, we need to accept our innate worth and appreciate the gifts God's given us to share with those around us.

As we age, our value doesn't diminish, even if our energy and the ability to do everything we once did starts to wan. In spite of mood swings, brain farts, and body parts that are heading south, we're every bit as valuable to others as we were back when our stomach was as taut as a trampoline. We need to be able to both give and receive within our circle of friends. And when we find ourselves alone, we need to know we're still in good company. That's the secret of friendship in a nutshell, regardless of what age (or how occasionally nutty) we are.

CHAPTER TEN

His Eye Is on the Sparrow, While Mine's on the Empty Nest

D o you have kids?" Right after we moved to Phoenix, my husband and I were asked this question over and over again.

"No," my husband would reply.

"Yes!" I'd quickly add, accompanied by the obligatory eye roll. "We have a son and a daughter, but they're grown and live in Colorado!"

How quickly a dad can forget. Once the nest is empty, it's all over but the college tuition. But for a mom, even one whose biddy brain can fog over in an instant, causing her to forget how her bra wound up in the vegetable crisper, we never fail to remember the fruit of our womb. Even if that fruit has matured and left the branch.

Granted, not every biddy experiences the typical empty nest phase. Some of us never have children. Some of our children have physical or emotional challenges that prevent them from heading out on their own. Sometimes our children head to heaven before we do, leaving behind a nest that always feels incomplete. For myriad different reasons, if this topic is a painful one, my heart breaks for you. But I encourage you to keep reading. You may discover something that will help you better understand, and empathize, with your fellow biddies who are facing this stage of life.

As for me, my nest emptied rather abruptly. My daughter graduated from high school a year early, robbing me of 365 days of maternal hovering. By then, my son had already moved into an apartment with friends. Shortly afterward, my husband was offered a job in Phoenix. So we picked up the nest and promptly moved it to another state. (Hint: this is one way to keep the kids from moving back in too easily!)

Okay, so we did provide a forwarding address—along with a plane ticket to come and visit during the holidays. Though it was more than a decade ago, I still remember that first morning of Thanksgiving break. I was up early, before anyone else. I stood on the landing of our new home, quietly basking in the bliss of looking at the closed guest room doors and knowing the guests inside were my very own sleeping children. Knowing they were home, safe and sound, under our roof, filled my heart with such a depth of peace and contentment that it immediately brought God to mind. I figured this is how He must feel once His children arrive in heaven: *Phew! The kids finally made it home. Safe at last!*

Of course, having my children under my roof doesn't ensure they'll be any safer than they are out on their own. But my mother's heart feels I can—and should—protect them, advise them, dry their tears, bear their burdens, bake them brownies, make them smile, lavish them with gifts, meddle in their affairs … You know, standard mother fare.

So when the nest is suddenly empty, we moms find ourselves out of a job. What's more, it's a job that feels custom made for who we are. Many women feel it's the most important, demanding, and fulfilling position they've ever held, and will hold, in their entire lives. Oh, sure. There's still mothering to come, but it's not the same. We've graduated to more of an advisory position. No wonder an empty nest can feel so much like an empty life.

HEAVY MEDDLE

For moms, the onset of the empty nest is like the final stage of delivery. Time to push our children out into the big, bright, beautiful world. But some of us cross our legs and refuse to let them go. We may be outwardly smiling as our children head off to college, married life, or a career. But behind the scenes, our apron strings double as octopus arms, firmly attaching their tentacles to every area of our children's young adult lives.

Technology has helped make this suction all the more secure. It used to be that when kids left home, all a mom could do was send homemade cookies and hope they'd answer the phone when she called. Today we can text anytime our kids come to mind. We can stalk their Facebook page, their Instagram pics, and their bank accounts, all courtesy of the Internet. We'd monitor their grades if colleges allowed us the freedom to hack their personal page. But they don't. Which is smart. Because our children are no longer children, regardless of how we picture them in our minds.

Maybe it's tough to let them go because this stage of life arrived with so little fanfare. At least for us. Sure, the kids got a graduation ceremony, congratulatory cards, and cash. We got more bills and an empty womb—uh … room. Or maybe it's not so empty. Maybe their former bedroom is a shrine, one we choose to worship at each morning as we pass by.

Consider how much time and energy we spent preparing for these same kids' arrival. We grilled our obstetrician, monitored what we ate, decorated the nursery, washed every newborn outfit in baby-safe detergent, installed nursery monitors, baby gates, childproof locks, and car seats. We read everything we could get our hands on about parenting and diligently practiced our Lamaze breathing.

What did we do to prepare for our children's departure? We helped them pack, gave them a hug, and said good-bye. It's no wonder it often takes a while to adjust to this "childless" phase of life. But adjust we must. Once our kids grow up, it's time for us to do the same. The time is over for living vicariously through our children's lives. All those things we said we'd do if we only had time come back to haunt us. We're stuck with a sudden revelation: we no longer have our kids as an excuse. We have to actually get a life. Our own.

The day my husband and I dropped our daughter off at college (then beat a hasty retreat to try and disguise the fact that we were blubbering like kindergartners on the first day of school), we stopped at a mall near our home. I happened to see a pair of bright red shoes in a store window. I'd always wanted a pair of red shoes. But they seemed like an extravagance. Something reserved for special occasions. Besides, they're what clowns wear.

But at that moment I made a decision. I was a new woman. I was walking a new path. And I decided I was going to walk that unfamiliar road with some spring, whimsy, and chutzpah in my step. Even if others thought I looked silly doing it.

I'd be lying if I said I never looked back, that I never missed my hands-on parenting days or never wanted to reach out and mom-handle my children into decisions I felt were more in their best interest than the ones they chose to make on their own. But in all fairness, Jesus felt the very same way.

As He looked out over Jerusalem, a city filled with God's wayward children, Jesus remarked, "O Jerusalem, Jerusalem, the city that kills the prophets and stones God's messengers! How often I have wanted to gather your children together as a hen protects her chicks beneath her wings, but you wouldn't let me" (Matthew 23:37 NLT). So what did Jesus do? He continued allowing those children the liberty to exercise the free will their heavenly Father gave them. The freedom to choose blessings or curses. The freedom to soar or stumble, to love or leave, to grow, to change, to begin again. And the promise that regardless of the choices those children make, their loving Parent will never turn His back on them or walk away.

If that approach to parenting is good enough for God, it should be good enough for empty nesters like us.

MAMMA MIA, HERE I GO AGAIN...

Grandma Mardel was a helicopter parent before helicopters were even invented. She proudly told me that she loved her only child, Frankie (my father), so much that she never, ever even dreamt of leaving him with a babysitter. Of course, she mentioned this as my husband and I were preparing to drop our kids off at a friend's house so we could head out on a date. From what I witnessed later in life, I believe Mardel's smothering mothering seriously backfired.

My father and his mother were like oil and water, only considerably more combustible. My childhood was littered with reoccurring blowups, after which my father would forbid us from ever seeing our grandmother again. This usually lasted only a week or so but continued to provide relational fireworks throughout the year, guaranteed to outshine the Fourth of July. When my grandmother moved out of state (to *my* state!) during the last six years of her life, my father only visited her once. That visit lasted less than an hour.

When my dad talked about his mother, he labeled her critical, manipulative, short-tempered, and a borderline psychotic. Funny thing is (or maybe not so funny), that's the exact same way I'd describe him. Coincidence? I think not. Sure, we all have free will. But we're also apt to pick up a few traits of those we spend time with along the way.

Ezekiel 16:44 says, "Everyone who quotes proverbs will quote this proverb about you: 'Like mother, like daughter'" (NIV). (The same undoubtedly holds true for mothers and sons.) We often think of these words as a compliment. But that's not how they're used in Scripture. The mother cited in Proverbs despised her husband and children. Her daughter not only followed in her mother's footsteps but "soon became even more depraved" than she was. What a legacy!

As our nest empties out and our kids head off on their own, our hands-on parenting days come to an end. But how we continue to live our lives continues to teach volumes. The "do what I say, not what I do" method of childrearing didn't work when our kids were small, and it won't work now that they're adults. Even as biddies, the choices we make, the words we speak, the way we treat others (especially those who may not treat us well) still influence our grown children as well as those little prayed-for gems of biddyhood—our grandchildren.

Grandkids are one of the most celebrated benefits of having reached the empty nest stage of life. They're also another important reason for us to provide footsteps worth following. Just look at how much the examples set by Kitty and Mardel influenced my own life. Proverbs 17:6 tells us, "Children's children are a crown to the aged, and parents are the pride of their children" (NIV). What a gift it is to our children and grandchildren to be women they can be proud of throughout every age and stage of life.

Of course, to have grandchildren we have to actually become grandmothers. That sounds a lot older than it is. The word conjures up images of stoop-shouldered matrons, their sparse pewter hair twisted up in a tight bun, driving like the woman in the closing scenes of *Ferris Bueller's Day Off*. But you and I are living proof that those days are past. Today, Grandma's more likely to be golfing or doing yoga than sitting in a rocker. But that doesn't mean she's any less interested in cuddling a newborn—just so long as it's not hers.

But we don't have to have grandchildren, or even children for that matter, to help teach those around us not to fear the years ahead. The world needs examples of how to grow older with grace, good humor, and a glint in our eye that says, "Expect the unexpected. This is gonna be good!" Think Nelson Mandela, Ruth Bader Ginsburg, Maya Angelou, and Mother Teresa.

The more we believe that what's ahead of us has as much potential for good as what's behind us, the more others will be drawn to spend time with us, to uncover the secret of the hope we hold. As for that once-empty nest, it's time we feathered it in a fresh new way with the love of grandchildren, grown children, and those we've taken under our wing with whom we have no familial ties at all, other than the ties of love.

CHAPTER ELEVEN

Living
La Diva Loca

I t's a good thing our nest empties out when it does. About that same time, there are often some old birds hankering to hop right in. Even if our aging parents don't literally move into our home, it's not uncommon for them to forward all of their emotional baggage to our address. Or at least it feels that way. A word to the wise—unpacking those bags entitles you to a free ticket to Crazy Town.

The ride this ticket provides differs for every biddy. Some get a cushy seat by a window on a fairly scenic route. Others get a three-legged stool in the cargo hold of the Insanity Express. Given my family tree, which seems to hold more than its fair share of conmen and bootleggers, is it any surprise that my journey leaned toward the latter?

My ticket was issued when my mom had a series of strokes at the not-so-over-the-hill age of sixty-nine. One of the changes this set in motion was my parents pulling up stakes and moving to a new address. Luckily, that address wasn't mine. However, I was part of the relocation operation.

If you recall the Schweppes Bitter Lemon incident from a few chapters back, you're already aware that my parents have some food issues. These aren't anything new. When I was in elementary school, Dad had such a HoHo addiction that Mom was forced to hide these chocolatey logs of goodness in secure locations around the house. That helped ensure my sister and I would still have some available for our lunchbox in the morning.

Donuts were another of Dad's preferred drugs of choice. He liked to eat them in bed, using the sheets as a handy-dandy napkin and crumb catcher. This led to a rather unpleasant experience when he was awakened in the middle of the night by a long trail of ants marching in a straight line right over his face. Not wanting to totally ruin a good night's sleep, Dad got up, grabbed a can of Raid, sprayed his pillowcase, and dusted the offending critters right off onto the carpet. Problem solved. My father fluffed his pillow, laid back down, and went right to sleep. Fortunately, he still woke up again the next morning.

However, my father's fondness for eating everything within reach made the discovery at their new home all the more surprising. My husband and I were trying to organize the garage, which if history repeated itself would never afford enough open space to actually house a motor vehicle.

On the top of a wobbly stack of moving boxes, we found one labeled, "Open Immediately: Refrigerated Perishables." This was three years after their move.

Did you know three-year-old eggs are as hollow as those you blow out to decorate at Easter? Refrigerated fruit cups eventually turn to neon-green slime? Antique lunchmeat takes on the appearance of an iridescent Frisbee? More entertaining than the scientific value of the specimens we found was my husband's reaction to actually touching them. The bottom of this big box of yuck had long since dissolved into cardboard goo, oozing into the box of bedding below. So as my husband stood on a chair, tossing what had once been a promising lunch into the open trash bag I held below, he emitted a sound that can only be equated with that of a distressed humpback whale.

From what I hear, my sister had almost that exact same reaction when she uncovered the identity of the long, dark shadows in the light fixture of the redwood sauna in my parents' former home—a stash of mummified HoHos.

If this much crazy can happen simply by helping parents move, imagine what can happen if we dare unpack some long-ignored emotional baggage. Trust me. It can be even less appealing than three-year-old lunchmeat.

THE RUT OF RELATIVITY

We're not the only ones getting older. Our parents are beating us to the finish line. Often, we don't have the liberty of standing on the sidelines and cheering them on as they head into that final lap. Instead, we're the ones carrying them. The transition from being cared for to becoming a caregiver is no time to play diva. (Besides, that role may be already taken by our aging mother.) It's time to gather our wits, our faith, our sense of humor, and all the grace and compassion we can muster. Because let's face it, finding old food in the garage is a picnic compared to the skeletons we're bound to find stuffed in the closet.

Even the most well-adjusted family can still harbor regrets, nurse old wounds, and leave important words unsaid. As for not-so-well-adjusted families, this season of life can get downright ugly, particularly when the stress of age-related issues, such as dementia or the cost of extended nursing care, enter the picture.

As I'm sure you're aware, the fastest way to feel young again is to hang out with your family of origin. In minutes, we slide right back into the tiny tennies we wore when we were kids. We say things, do things, and even feel things that would be totally out of character if we were hanging out with our friends. But we're not. We're stuck in a time warp, a rut of relativity that's dug so deep it's very difficult to change. Especially when it comes to the ways we communicate with one another.

Personally, I'm rather partial to the hydrangea method of communication. I love flowers, but I've always been a bit of a grim reaper when it comes to gardening. That's why hydrangeas and I get along so well. When they're thirsty they droop over, their little heads bent straight down to the ground. Give them water and they perk up in no time, blossoms pointing heavenward once more. Hydrangeas are clear about what they want and respond instantly when they get what they need. If only family was that easy to read.

If our parents' little heads begin to droop, they could be angry, in prayer, depressed, bored, disapproving, embarrassed, or taking an unexpected nap. Even when they use their words to communicate, we may need a code talker to discern what they really mean. Of course, if I'm not careful, these words could just as easily describe me. That's why when it comes to family, I need to be tenaciously intentional about communicating the truth in love instead of glossing over the truth out of habit.

To get out of a rut, we first need to be fully aware of the one we're in. What ruts of miscommunication fit your family as snugly as a teenager's tube top? Is anger or silence used to control conversations? Are there any pesky pachyderms in the room that are off limits to discuss? Are problems buried alive instead of talked through? Do different rules apply to different members of the family?

I was aware of the intricate tango of communication within my immediate family, having danced it for years, but when I became a caregiver for Grandma Mardel, I quickly learned I'd have to master a whole new set of steps. One lesson came courtesy of running water. As Mardel was leaving the bathroom, I said offhandedly, "Grandma, you forgot to turn off the faucet." Being a mother with two small children at the time, I said this kind of thing repeatedly during the day, so I didn't give my comment any more thought. Until I received a handwritten, multipage letter later that week.

In it, Mardel expressed her shock, anger, and inconsolable hurt over how a granddaughter she'd lavished her love on for so many years could treat her like she was an imbecile in front of her very own great-grandchildren. Mardel emphasized, and reemphasized, what a disappointment I was and what a fool she'd been to mistakenly believe I loved her, when apparently all these years it was just an act.

Wow. Who knew running water could be that volatile of a topic? In retrospect, I should have known. A long-standing family rut was to never correct my father, so it should have come as no surprise to find that his mother was the one who'd helped furrow that original ditch.

So I tweaked my communication. I apologized to Mardel in person, not via letter. I affirmed my love for her. If the faucet was left running, I simply turned it off. I didn't correct her in public. But if I felt I needed to call her on something that mattered, I'd sit down with her in private and try and talk it out. I wasn't going to give her a free pass to say and do whatever she pleased. That wasn't how we communicated with our children, and I didn't want my kids sliding into any ruts I'd worked hard to climb out of.

In my younger days, I wholeheartedly believed any

relational problem could be resolved by simply talking it out. Unfortunately, this isn't always possible. Some people have no interest in exiting a rut they're in. They're comfortable with dysfunction. They'd rather end a relationship than admit they're wrong. For them, there's no meeting halfway. It's their way or the highway. At that point, all you can do is pray and let them go their own way.

If your aging parents fall into this category, and especially if you find yourself in a caregiver role, my wholehearted suggestion is to spring for a counselor. For you. Your parents would probably never listen to one. We need a voice of reason to remind us that we're not crazy. Our life is. We can only do crazy in small doses—and with a lot of outside support!

HONORING FAMILY TIES

I took a personality test once. Not to see if I had one, but to see what kind of career I was best suited for. The result? It recommended I *not* work with children or the elderly. At the time, I was raising two elementary-school-aged kids and was floundering my way through nine years of caring for my two grandmothers. No wonder there were days I felt tempted to pluck myself bald-headed. I wasn't well suited to the task. That didn't change the fact that this task was mine to do.

Being a caregiver for children, parents, grandparents, or any other human being who needs our help can be

CHAPTER TWELVE

Where's My Happily Ever After?

I was a mere whippersnapper at the time, forty-eight years young. Life was good. My son was getting married. My daughter was graduating from high school. My kids had big plans for the future—and so did I.

Perimenopause hadn't yet reared its ugly gray head. I was feeling older but not yet "old." I had a great circle of friends, a steady stream of writing contracts, lived in my dream house overlooking Pikes Peak, and was married to my best friend. I know. Nauseatingly perfect, right? Until over dinner one evening when my husband asked, "So, what would you think about moving to Phoenix?"

My reply? "Certainly God would not move us from heaven to hell!"

But He did.

And I'm forever grateful. I can say that from where I

stand now, ten years down the road. But back then if felt like the end of the world. My perfect world, anyway.

I'd felt that end-of-the-world heartache before. When a Greyhound bus left my mother and me behind at a rest stop and drove off with my teddy bear. When my pet rabbit died. When I wasn't chosen to be on the high school drill team. When a friend betrayed me. When my mother had a stroke. When Grandma Kitty died. Different seasons, different kinds of grief, but all devastating in their own unique way.

On the scale of potentially apocalyptic circumstances, losing a teddy bear or moving a couple of states away for a new job doesn't rise all that high. But it can feel like it does when it happens to you. I place part of the blame on fairy tales. Ever since we were small, we've been led to believe there's a magic slipper, a Prince Charming, our very own castle, and a happily ever after waiting for us just down the road.

By now, we've been on that road quite awhile. We've discovered it's filled with ups and downs, dead ends and detours, potholes and wrong turns. In other words, not so magical. So if prayers are not magic wishes, God and a fairy godmother are not synonymous, and being married to Prince Charming has its not-so-charming days, how do we hold on to hope? That depends on what we're hoping for.

Instead of longing to slip our foot into a fairy tale glass slipper, let's mentally walk in someone else's shoes for just a moment. It's a small tattered shoe, a child's shoe, worn during the bombing raids of World War II. Imagine what it would have been to like to be orphaned, starving, and then rescued and placed in a refugee camp. You'd think children would believe their happily ever after had finally arrived. But many of them were so traumatized by what had happened that they couldn't sleep. They were afraid they'd wake up to find it had all been a dream, that they were still alone, homeless, and hungry.

Even at a very young age, it was hard for these children to get out of a rut that had been deeply carved into their lives. So, what did their caregivers do? At bedtime, they gave each child a piece of bread to hold onto while he or she slept. It was a touchstone, a reminder that, "Today, I ate." It was also a promise, "Tomorrow, I will eat again."[1]

When we go to sleep every evening, are we holding tightly onto yesterday and mistaking it for bread? Our past carves ruts in us all. Some of them are destructive, leading us farther away from God and from who He created us to be. We may have traveled these ruts for so long that we erroneously believe they're the only path available to us. But we have a choice. Remember Deuteronomy 30:19? Before us lay life and death, blessings and curses. Some of these options, both the good and the bad, lay ahead of us precisely because of what lies behind us.

---

1 Dennis Linn, Sheila Fabricant Linn, and Matthew Linn, *Sleeping with Bread: Holding What Gives You Life* (New York: Paulist Press, 1995), 1.

GET OVER IT OR YOU'LL
NEVER GET OUT FROM UNDER IT

"Pack up all your troubles in an old kit-bag and smile, smile, smile!" Does that chorus ring a bell? (Not that I'm insinuating you or I were born back when it was written in 1915. We may be old, but we're not centenarians … yet!) This song became a popular anthem during the first World War. The chorus may be catchy, but the message makes for lousy lifestyle advice. In retrospect, I'm certain the two brothers who wrote the song, George and Felix Powers, would agree. Their stepbrother died on the battlefield in WWI. Later, after fighting in WWII, Felix committed suicide.

When it comes to hauling around heavy emotional baggage, "grin and bear it" doesn't do us any favors. It's not choosing life. It's choosing denial. Funny thing is, the memories we'd most like to forget are the ones that stick with us like a pesky wad of chewing gum on our orthopedic pumps. We may not remember where we put our car keys five minutes ago, but we can recall every word of a friend's betrayal from way back in grade school.

The truth is, we're hardwired this way. The more emotional an event, the more deeply it's embedded in our brains. This isn't a cruel joke courtesy of creation. It's a gift. Really. Tough times can be top-notch teachers—if we choose to listen. We can learn what *not* to do in the future. We can become more empathetic, wiser in knowing how to help those who walk a similarly bumpy path.

Personally, I believe another reason God ensures these kind of memories stick with us is to force us to act on them. Make amends. Repent. Forgive someone, including ourselves. Typically, this doesn't happen all at once. Bits and pieces of heartache dislodge from our lives one small shard at a time. But the Biddy Years are the perfect time to get serious about unpacking any emotional odds and ends we're still lugging around.

In *The Wisdom of Menopause*, Dr. Christiane Northrup tells us, "Biologically, at this stage of life you are programmed to withdraw from the outside world for a period of time and revisit your past."[2] Revisiting is fine. We just don't want to take up permanent residence there.

Once we learn from and act on what's weighing us down, it's time to pull an Elsa and let it go. Journal. Pray. Picture putting past wounds in God's healing hands. Ask for outside help from a pastor or counselor if needed. But if hopelessness and heartache just won't let go, talk to your physician. You may be the one out of ten people who suffer from depression. Asking for help, and taking medication if needed, doesn't mean you're weak. It means you're wise and proactive.

When it comes to our mental health and how we deal with the past, we choose whether we'll play the role of victim or victor. We can't change what's happened to us. But

---

2   Christiane Northrup, MD, *The Wisdom of Menopause* (New York: Bantam Books, 2006), 46.

we can change how we look at it—and how we look at ourselves in light of it.

Back when I was in college and was accepted to the foreign study program, I remember sharing the good news with Grandma Mardel. I anticipated a hearty congratulations but instead received a rather spirited tongue lashing. "How can you possibly consider going to Italy for ten months?" she snapped. "Why, I could die!"

Hint: This is not what's meant by the catchphrase "Live like you're dying." This is playing the role of self-centered victim. Mardel's death threat was two decades premature. But that didn't stop her from repeating it any time I was about to embark on an adventure that took me away from her immediate vicinity. For my grandmother, my absence was just another bad thing happening to her. It didn't matter if it was good for me.

Mardel clung tightly to her victim role and stayed there for as long as I can remember. (Perhaps that's why she slept with loaded pistols under each of the four corners of her mattress at the retirement home. Well, at least she did until the staff came to change the sheets.) If Mardel told you her life story, it would be tragedy from beginning to end. I don't believe she thought she could have a "happily ever after," because in Mardel's eyes, she'd never experienced a happy "once upon a time." She didn't see herself as blessed but cursed. It was her long-term rut of choice. So in Deuteronomy 30:19 terms, she continued to choose death instead of life over and over again. Even when life was spread out like a banquet before her.

Victim or victor. Life or death. The stakes are high when it comes to the choices we make. Our happily ever after begins with the moment we're living right now. How happy will our tomorrow be? Once again, the choice is ours.

HAPPINESS IS A DIY PROJECT

Change is in the wind. Again. From where I stand right now, it looks rather big and scary. I'm straining to see that light at the end of the tunnel, but it isn't quite in sight. Yet. So it's a good thing I have a secret weapon. It isn't a time machine, a cloak of invisibility, a pistol under my mattress, or a gooey chocolate cake with only one fork.

It's a kitchen towel.

I'm not here to sing the praises of its absorbency or tell you how you can distract yourself from whatever difficult situation you're going through by cleaning house. It's what's written on the towel that matters. It reads: Today I will be happier than a bird with a french fry.

I've eaten on the patio at In-N-Out Burger. I've watched the birds—their eyes on the prize—wait for a family to leave without thoroughly cleaning their table. I've seen them nab a discarded fry and dance around like Pharrell Williams to his "Happy" song. Those birds aren't regretting the fry they missed yesterday or worrying about what's on the menu tomorrow. They're reveling in the yumminess of here and now.

Even on the darkest of days, we can find at least one french fry worth a dance step or two—if we look for it. Happiness is really all about where we choose to look.

Philippians 4:4 says, "Rejoice in the Lord always" (NIV). But it doesn't stop there. For us absentminded biddies it provides a quick recap. "I will say it again: Rejoice!" Lots of folks throw this verse around like a pair of rose-colored glasses prescribed by God. But this verse isn't telling us to suck it up, "smile, smile, smile," and pretend cod liver oil is a tasty french fry. The apostle Paul isn't finished with his point quite yet.

He continues, "Let your gentleness be evident to all. The Lord is near. Do not be anxious about anything, but in every situation, by prayer and petition, with thanksgiving, present your requests to God. And the peace of God, which transcends all understanding, will guard your hearts and your minds in Christ Jesus. Finally, brothers and sisters, whatever is true, whatever is noble, whatever is right, whatever is pure, whatever is lovely, whatever is admirable—if anything is excellent or praiseworthy—think about such things" (Philippians 4:5–8 NIV).

Happiness is an inside job. And it begins in our mind. To rejoice means to find delight in something. When we find delight, we discover thankfulness snuggled up right next door. As we focus on searching out, and thinking about, the beautiful, positive gifts we have in life, our gratitude can't help but grow. The more it grows, the lighter our hearts become and the more french fries we'll find that we spy along the way.

Will we live happily ever after? Not like in the movies. Real life has its ups and its downs. Some will experience the relatively mild thrills and spills of a roller coaster ride. For others, the so-called golden years will hold the unexpected and unwelcome … financial pitfalls, chronic health issues, the end of a marriage, the death of those we love. Their over-the-hill journey may feel more like clinging to an out-of-control skateboard as it heads right over the edge of the Grand Canyon.

How we decide to tell our story, to others as well as to ourselves, will help determine our trajectory on the happily-ever-after scale—regardless of our circumstances. Will we view the coming season through the lens of tragedy or as a God-inspired tale of adventure? Will we give up the ghosts of our past or cling to them as part of our identity? Will we narrate our tale as victors or victims? Will we "sleep with bread" and live "hope-ily" ever after?

In the words of Ralph Waldo Emerson, "Tomorrow is a new day. You shall begin it well and serenely and with too high a spirit to be cumbered with your old nonsense." Vicki's version: Fellow Biddies, let's write a new chapter instead of rereading the past—while keeping our eyes peeled for french fries along the way!

CHAPTER THIRTEEN

You Can Teach an Old Broad New Tricks

I t was 11 p.m. and raining. I'd been standing outside for hours in skintight pants and a turquoise tutu. Of course, you couldn't see my classy ensemble because over the top of it all was a plastic garbage bag with a hole for my head torn in the top. Time for some family fun. Sorta.

The "fun" hadn't even really begun. I still had to walk 13.1 miles. In the dark. In the cold. In the rain. In a glitter-covered tutu. Everyone around me ran, including my husband, daughter, and son-in-law. But my knees gave up that nonsense long ago. At my age, I only run in case of fire or to catch up with an ice cream truck. So, less than a minute after crossing the starting line, my family disappeared into the crowd of more than 12,000 other misguided souls who'd actually paid for the privilege of racing through the back lots of Disney World in the middle of the night.

Family bonding over. Tedium, just getting started.

Honestly, I enjoy walking. Always have. But I hate competition. I don't even like to play board games with people who care if they win or lose. My daughter assured me there'd be lots of people who'd be walking instead of running and that I'd only be in competition with myself. But everyone else was racing past me like a herd of crazed gazelles. Gazelles wearing mouse ears, tiaras, and trash bags, that is.

I continued plodding along at my own pedestrian pace. Four miles later, thanks to the incessant drizzle and Orlando humidity, my trash bag transformed into a terrarium. I tore it off before mushrooms had a chance to sprout in my cleavage. Within minutes, my entire body was as wet as my soggy socks.

As I hoofed it through Animal Kingdom, the drizzle turned to a downpour. I kept careful watch to make certain animals weren't beginning to pair themselves up two by two. I was also on the lookout for a biddy's best friend—a convenient bathroom. As we all know, a biddy bladder, like a furtive firefly, is most active at night. Already anxious about keeping under the required sixteen-minute-mile pace, I attempted the world's fastest bathroom break.

Unfortunately, I hadn't anticipated the difficulty of trying to break the suction of wet runner's tights clinging to my thighs like barnacles to a blue whale. Let's just say that no records were broken that night. By me, at least.

But despite the nonstop deluge, aching muscles, and a rather spectacular tumble on a wet grate that landed me right on my tutu in a gritty puddle, I crossed the finish line in three hours, twenty-nine minutes, and fifty-four seconds (six seconds to spare!), leaving behind a 13.1-mile trail of glitter in the mud.

When our family reunited at the finish line, we snapped our obligatory photo wearing our oversized medals, proof of how absolutely foolhardy and tenacious we really are. When I look at that photo today, I can't help but notice how much I resemble a deranged ventriloquist's dummy with my wide smile, my hair plastered flat on my head, and my cheeks flushed neon red. But there's something else I can't help but notice. It's the fact that I accomplished something I never dreamed I could do—least of all during my Biddy Years.

STARTING A SECOND ACT WHEN YOU'RE PRAYING FOR A SECOND WIND

According to my mailbox, I've already got one foot in the grave. Along with my AARP magazine, I receive ads for long-term health care insurance, invitations to test how likely I am to suffer from heart disease, coupons to use toward the purchase of a motorized scooter, and catalogues filled with handy-dandy aids, such as salad tong–like arm extenders so I can pull up my socks without actually having to get anywhere near my own feet.

Add the travel itineraries for "active senior" tours to Branson and limited time offers for compression socks, and there's enough evidence for any court in the land to convict me of impersonating an "old" person. Because one thing's for sure: I'm sure not going to let them accuse me of actually being one.

If cats have nine lives, certainly God gave those of us created in His image many more. He's given us the ability—and freedom—to reinvent ourselves over and over again. That's what daring to climb out of an obsolete or ill-fitting rut is all about.

Look at Moses. He died at the age of 120 after leading those whiney Israelites through the desert for forty years. That means he was eighty when he led them across the Red Sea. Did Moses have second thoughts about his second act? You bet. Right from the start, Moses told God he didn't feel up to the task. Insecure about his own speaking ability, Moses deferred to Aaron to be his mouthpiece. Moses continued to second-guess himself throughout his season of leadership, but that didn't stop him from accomplishing some amazing stuff along the way.

The Bible isn't the only place where we find older people doing extraordinary things. At the age of seventy-five, Barbara Hillary became one of the oldest individuals, and the first African-American woman, to reach the North Pole. At the age of eighty-eight, Helen Hooven Santmyer became a best-selling author. Heart surgeon Michael DeBakey patented a groundbreaking surgical procedure at the age of ninety. At ninety-three, Betty White's acting career is still going strong. Orchestra conductor Leopold Stokowski signed a six-year recording contract at the age of ninety-four. Compared to Stokowsi, Colonel Sanders was still a spring you-know-what when he founded Kentucky Fried Chicken at seventy-two.

Chances are we're still younger than the majority of the innovators listed above. That means, God willing, we've still got time for not only a second act, but a third, a fourth … who knows how many inventions and reinventions in our lifetime. Of course, that depends on what we choose to do with the time God sets before us.

There's a famous sketch of a very old man, bearded, bent, and leaning heavily on a cane in each hand as he struggles to walk. Drawn by the Spanish artist Goya (at the age of eighty), it's entitled *I Am Still Learning*. That's the key. As long as we're still learning, we're still growing, still changing, still in the process of painting the full portrait of the woman God created us to be.

But to have a second act there has to be *act*ion. God designed our body and brain to work together to make this happen. How we think can change the way we behave. But it also works the other way around. How we choose to behave can change how we think, which can cause the neurons in our brain to actually grow and change. Yes, even at our ever-advancing age.

Sure, our biddy brains may be shrinking in size, and we may experience mental misfires now and again, but this doesn't mean we're dumbing down. Michael J. Gelb writes in *Brain Power: Improve Your Mind As You Age* (co-authored with Kelly Howell, a leading innovator in applying brainwave research to real life), "The brain is not, as was once thought, a compartmentalized static machine whose parts eventually wear out. Instead it is a highly adaptable and dynamic organ, capable of generating new neurons and improving as we get older."[1]

Improving. Yup, you read that right. One action that has been scientifically proven to change our brain, and our life, for the better is prayer. Short little "gimme" prayers, saying grace at mealtime, or reciting a rote prayer before we hit the hay doesn't register on a brain scan. However, as little as twelve minutes of focused, contemplative prayer over the course of eight weeks alters our brain in such a significant way that a brain scan can measure the change. As a result of this change, our brain pushes us to become stronger in our compassion toward others and in our ability to hold our irrationally emotional urges at bay.[2] This is great news for hormonally challenged biddies!

---

1 Marilyn Preston, "Like a Fine Wine, Brain Can Improve with Age," *Arizona Republic*, March 2, 2012.
2 Rob Moll, *What Your Body Knows About God*, (Downers Grove, IL: IVP Books, 2014), 15, 26.

It's also great news when it comes to reinvention. In the words of that great BBC time-traveling alien theologian, Doctor Who, "We're all stories in the end. Write a good one." If parts of my brain can be rewritten, so can the upcoming chapters of my life.

REBEL WITHOUT APPLAUSE

Here are just a few of the things (besides a half marathon) I've tried for the first time after the age of fifty: paddle boarding, Pilates, shrimp and grits, starting up a photography ministry, throwing pottery (not literally, though that might be therapeutic during certain estrogen-starved moments of mayhem), painting, writing fiction, and cooking with a tagine. Oh yeah, and walking coast to coast—two hundred miles—across Great Britain.

I also tried Zumba, but when buzzards started circling my car every time I drew close to the gym, I switched to Pilates. Not everything we try we'll enjoy or will turn out be a whopping success. I tried to work up to running the half marathon, but my knees were very clear in communicating that was a very bad idea. So I listened. And I walked.

The good news is that at our age, we don't have to worry as much about the embarrassment of failure. Because frankly, no one's watching. The older we get, the more invisible we become, especially to those who are younger than we are. Their expectations of what we can do are very low. When kids below the age of forty see me, they see Whistler's

Mother in more contemporary clothes. They picture me sitting in a rocking chair and knitting by the fireside. When they hear I walked across Great Britain, they act as though I swam the British Channel. Who knows? Maybe someday I will. Or not. It all depends on where I decide to direct my time, my energy, and my passion.

Did you know Whistler's mother was only sixty-seven when her son painted that famous portrait? I remember seeing *Arrangement in Gray and Black No. 1* (the painting's official title) at the Louvre back when I was a college student. Unfortunately, the museum guard from whom I asked to borrow a chair, so I could "pose" in front of the painting for a photo, did not share my unique take on art appreciation. So I spent some time simply staring at Whistler's mom, giving her a careful once-over. She looked old. Shriveled. Fragile. Bored to tears. I could almost hear her saying, "James Abbott McNeill Whistler, would you get on with it? My lumbago is acting up!" But one thing is certain. That woman wasn't in a rush because she was late for a Pilates class.

Sixty-seven ain't what it used to be. Neither is fifty-seven or eighty-seven. Today, biddies can feel free to get a college degree, volunteer for the Peace Corps, take electric guitar lessons or, like Diana Nyad, swim from Cuba to Florida at the age of sixty-four—or beyond.

Granted, if we want to embark on a new career at this point, we're liable to smack our little heads against a gray ceiling as well as a glass one. Age discrimination is alive and well. But competence, persistence, and flexibility on our part can take us far. It can lead us places that were never even on the map of our future as we pictured it back in the days of our early adulthood.

However, not all second acts are a matter of choice. Some are thrust upon us. As we'll talk about in the next chapter, an unwelcome change in marital status, our financial picture, or our overall health can force us down an unexpected road. But we still have that Deuteronomy 30:19 choice of life or death, blessings or curses.

What will we do with what we have to work with? Consider artist Frida Kahlo. Sure, she was only a teen when she was in a debilitating accident. But it was that accident that led her to start painting to pass the time. The rest is art history. Who knows what fabulous second act may begin from what appeared to us to be the end?

Both of my grandmothers were forced into a second act when they moved out of their own homes and into a care facility. Grandma Kitty was grateful for her new little place and the new people she met. Even when her dementia made it difficult to remember why she was where she was, she voiced over and over again how thankful she was to be there. What Grandma Mardel voiced over and over again would not be printable in this book.

During the last three years of her life, Kitty got to really know her great-grandkids. In turn, they had the privilege of getting to know and love her. Those three years weren't easy for our family, and certainly not for her, but we wouldn't have missed out on Kitty's second act for the world. She taught us all so much, even if she had no idea of what an amazing teacher she was. Her presence made a positive difference in all of our lives.

We never know when, like Kitty, our second act will become our final act. So instead of making a Bucket List of what we want to do, let's make a Becoming List of who we want to be. For me, walking a half marathon was part of that. I want to be active so I can play with my grandkids instead of just watching them play. Focusing on God in contemplative prayer also plays an important part. I want to change my brain in more beneficial, compassionate ways so I can love well. How about you? Who do you want to grow up to be—and how do you plan on getting there?

Longevity can be the mother of reinvention, an invitation for a spectacular second act, or it can be a boring, bitter slide toward our finale. As always, the choice is ours. And the time to make that choice is now. Bitter or better … Which will you choose?

CHAPTER FOURTEEN

God Is Expanding Along with my Waistline

God and I almost had a knockdown, drag-out tussle over a permanent marker. Right there in church. It was a Sunday in January, the perfect time for New Year's resolutions and fresh commitments. Our pastor's challenge was to put ourselves in the disciples' shoes and take a fresh look at Jesus. As a visible reminder of our commitment, we were asked to sign our name on a large white board that would remain in the church sanctuary throughout the year.

Waiting in line for my turn to sign, I held an internal debate over which color marker I should choose out of the buckets placed in front of the board. Purple? My favorite, a sign of royalty, perfect for a King's kid—or a King's biddy.

Orange? Bright, bold, not afraid to be seen. Green? A symbol of new growth. So many choices, so little time.

But when I got up to the board, the thoughtful man in front of me handed me the marker he'd used. It was black. Common, boring, pencil-lead, burnt-toast, lump-of-coal black. Not only that, it looked dried out, used up, hardly fit for the privileged task at hand. That's when the battle began.

I didn't want to be impolite by refusing the marker given to me or hold up the line by digging through the bucket for a brighter, more playfully colored marker (you know, an implement that more accurately represented me!). But the matter seemed out of my hands once that black marker was in it. I signed my dull gray, almost indiscernible signature. Then I grumbled and tussled with God all the way back to my seat and throughout the prayer time that followed.

I knew it was stupid and petty. Perhaps it even bordered on psychotic. But I whined a prayer about how unhappy I was to sign with a marker devoid of color. After all, choosing to follow God back when I was eighteen always reminded me of the movie *The Wizard of Oz*. When I opened the door of my heart to God, my life was transformed from black and white into technicolor.

That's when I started to cry. Could have been hormones. Could have been the Holy Spirit. Always hard to tell at this point in my life. Always hard to tell at this point in my life. Regardless, I pleaded, *So, God, considering how You've changed my world for the better, why do I go around with a broken heart so much of the time?*

That's when God answered back. Not audibly, mind you. Not written on the white board with a disembodied hand, like the message Daniel read at King Belshazzar's shindig in the Old Testament. It was more of an "Aha!" kind of moment. One where you feel God whisper something in your heart and mind that is so unexpected, so contrary to what you'd usually think or say, that you feel it has to be from heaven above. The words I attributed to Him were, "Haven't you prayed to have a heart like Mine?"

The tears stopped and so did my whiney rant. I considered so many things that must break God's heart, over and over again. War, abuse, betrayal, hate … Not one of them involved a felt-tipped marker.

GOD-IN-THE-BOX

What does God, and the character of His heart, look like to you? It's tough to provide a solid, accurate picture of a spiritual, infinite being. Here's Someone we can't see or hear or touch. We can't relate to Him in the same way we relate to everyone else we've ever met. Even if we could, God is so big in every sense of the word that ultimately He's beyond the comprehension of our finite human brains, even when they're not menopausally misfiring.

But we don't want an incomprehensible God. We want answers. We want black and white, right and wrong, without a hint of gray. We want a God-in-the-Box, preferably with a drive-thru. Then we can swing by when it's convenient, order what we want, and expect it'll be delivered just the way we like it. Our way. Hold the condemnation, heavy on the grace. At least as far as it applies to us.

We may not admit it, even to ourselves, but we don't want to live with mystery. We want exactly what Adam and Eve did. We want to eat from the tree of knowledge (though we'd prefer a truffle tree to an apple tree, if possible) and become just like God. We want comprehension and control. But as the Rolling Stones remind us, "You can't always get what you want." And the Biddy Years are the perfect time to come to grips with that truth—and relish the freedom that comes when we accept it.

I think most of us assumed that by the time we had our AARP card in hand, we'd have it all figured out … life, love, and faith. But if we're honest with ourselves, and with God, chances are we have more questions and fewer answers than we did when we were younger. One reason is that God has gotten bigger over the years. Not because of hormonal or dietary issues. But the closer we draw to God, the bigger we realize He is. It's like when we see a mountain in the distance. It looks like a small hill on the horizon, something easily conquerable—until we get close to it. Only then do we realize its true size and how insurmountable it really is.

Since our ever-expanding God will continue to break out of every box we try and squeeze Him into, we only have three options. First, we can refuse to hang out with a God who doesn't play by our rules. We can dump Him like an outdated minivan in our midlife crisis of faith. Then we can set out to find a brand-new, shiny red sports car of spirituality. There's even a website to help us. By answering a few faith-based questions on Belief-O-Matic on beliefnet.com, we can discover if we're better suited to be a Buddhist than a Baptist.

Another option is to fashion God in our own image. We can make certain God hates the same people we hate but loves us just the way we are. We can treat Scripture like a fortune cookie, picking and choosing individual verses that support our way of thinking while throwing out the ones we disagree with or don't understand. We can become more dogmatic in how we live what we've chosen to believe, distrustful of anyone who dares to ask a question. That includes ourselves.

Our final choice is to accept that when it comes to God, we'll never understand it all—and that tomorrow we may understand even less than we thought we did today. We can be willing to say, "I was wrong" or "I don't know." We can give up trying to play God's defense attorney and simply be His witness, willing to share with others what we've seen God do firsthand in our own lives.

We can be the Martin Luther of our own faith, refusing to accept the way things are just because that's the way they've always been. As we mature, we can change how we live out our faith, just like the church has done over the years. At one time the church supported slavery, drowned those suspected of witchcraft, and castrated young boys to make a more melodious choir. It condemned dancing, drinking, divorce, and remarriage. But people were willing to take a second look, to reconsider, to question the status quo. Things changed. So can we.

My Grandma Kitty was very strict in her Catholic faith. For years she prayed I would come to a true faith in God, long after I'd done exactly that at a Young Life camp at the age of eighteen. But when she was in her late eighties, my grandmother came to me and said, "You know what? I think you and I believe the same thing!"

Both God and I broke out of the box she tried to put us in. But Kitty didn't ignore us, walk away from us, or try her best to shove us back in. She humbly embraced us, and change, with open arms. That's the kind of biddy I want to be.

THE ROAD FROM ODD TO AWED

I almost got kicked out of a Bible study once. Apparently, all the questions I asked were upsetting the other women. At least that's what the leader said when she confronted me. Personally, I think my questions were upsetting the leader more than the other women, because she felt she had to have an answer for them all, especially those that called into question the parochial statements the study made. From my perspective, her God was too small.

God is plenty big to handle our questions, our doubts, our misconceptions, our arrogance, and even our menopausal mood swings. We aren't odd or irreverent when we struggle to make sense out of Scripture, out of God, or out of this incredibly quirky thing called life. As we approach biddydom, that struggle can get all the more volatile. Sure, our brain is being rewired and we're retaining every fluid we've imbibed for the last seven days. But we're also more aware of how fleeting time is. We want to make certain we're headed the right direction, because the time we have left to turn around and rechart our course is growing shorter every day.

It's little wonder that the older we get, the more we tend to pray. The Pew Research Center reports that 48 percent of Americans between the ages of eighteen and twenty-nine pray every day. When those youngsters reach the early Biddy Years of fifty to fifty-nine, that percentage grows to 61 percent. Those over the age of seventy who have daily conversations with God average around 70 percent.[1]

Prayer isn't just an American thing or even a Christian thing. Anthropologists contend that prayer is one of the earliest recorded human behaviors. Even those who say they don't believe in God still pray on occasion. Crying out for help when we're afraid, in pain, or in need feels perfectly natural. Even if we don't believe there's anyone out there to hear.

---

1 Bill Newcott, "The Paradox of Prayer," *AARP Magazine*, February/March 2015, 49.

But there's one kind of prayer that changes us, and our lives, for the better. And it's one that doesn't even require words. This prayer bubbles up unexpectedly, often arriving right out of the blue. That blue could be the ocean, a vibrant summer sky, or a bluebird perched right outside our window. It could be any color of the rainbow—or a literal rainbow for that matter! From the artistic sweep of the day's fading light to the sound of a newborn's cry, there are countless things in this world that make our hearts swell with joy and wonder. That inspire awe.

Awe is an amazing little sensation. It's sparked by beauty, mystery, and wonders we can't fully comprehend or explain. Unlike other pleasures we enjoy, such as eating a gooey caramel brownie, winning at Scrabble, or laughing at a late-night movie, awe doesn't engage the me-focused part of our brains. It draws us toward being more we-focused. It sparks a flood of oxytocin, a hormone that helps us feel more connected with others.[2] Including God.

This is why when something takes our breath away, we want to share that experience with those around us. We may post a pic on Facebook, point it out to a total stranger, or simply find ourselves overcome with thanks and praise— offering a full-body prayer to God. I remember watching an awe-inspiring sunset with a crowd of strangers at the Grand Canyon. As the final light faded, people began to

---

2   David Hochman, "The Wonder of It All," *Oprah* magazine, December 2010, 153.

applaud. That standing ovation was prayer at its finest, a spontaneous gift of gratitude and worship.

As burgeoning biddies, getting older forces us to slow down. What a gift! If we decide to use it, that is. The more slowly we walk, the more wonders we notice and the more awe we're likely to encounter along the way. Becoming more attuned to awe in our lives can lead us to feel more fulfilled and connected, to become more aware of how we play an integral part in God's remarkable world. It lifts our spirits and inspires us to be more compassionate toward others. It's what makes singing together at church, or even at a rock concert, invoke a powerful emotional response in us. We sense we're part of something bigger than ourselves.

On even the most ordinary of days, we're surrounded by miracles and mystery. Instead of feeling the need to explain it, control it, or cram it back into a mental box, we can choose to welcome it, rest in it, and celebrate it with others, including the Author of mystery, God Himself. As Albert Einstein warned, "Do not grow old, no matter how long you live. Never cease to stand like curious children before the great mystery into which you were born."

Stay curious, my friend. It's a life changer. There's mystery, wonder, and awe ahead. We don't have to understand it all to anticipate the gift of it all. God is big and so are His plans for us. And those plans aren't finished yet.

CHAPTER FIFTEEN

The Trojan Hearse

When I was a kid, I dreamed of becoming an archaeologist. This career choice was heavily inspired by the book mobile. Being an avid reader, and perhaps a tad OCD, I started reading my way through the van's limited collection beginning with the "A" shelf. Hence, archaeology.

One of the first books I read was an account of Heinrich Schliemann's discovery of the ancient city of Troy. And yes, this is very geeky reading for an elementary school child. But my itty-bitty brain, before it grew up, grew old, and transformed into a biddy brain, was drawn to studying old ruins and fossils. Talk about full circle. That's exactly what I'm doing now. Only currently that fossil is me. But I digress. Back to Troy…

The reason a city built in northwestern Turkey twenty-seven centuries ago is still familiar to us is due to Homer's literary classics, *The Illiad* and *The Odyssey* (and no, I did not read these in grammar school). Remember the story about the Greeks building a humongous wooden horse, pretending it's a gift for the people of Troy? When night fell, the soldiers hiding inside that "gift" descended on the city of Troy and destroyed it.

In my addled little cranium, I picture the last chapter of my Biddy Years ending with a Trojan Hearse. Think Trojan Horse—only in reverse. Where the Trojan Horse appeared to be a gift but instead brought death and destruction, a Trojan Hearse looks like anything but a gift, especially for the guest of honor riding inside. It appears to carry death. The End. But like the horse, the hearse is not what it seems. Death carries with it its own unique gift—not the end, but a new beginning, a promise of heaven and eternal life.

All of this sounds simply spectacular. A storybook ending fitting the power and creativity of the Author of Life. But how do we know what we read in the Bible about heaven is true? Chances are pretty good that the Trojan Horse is just a myth. No evidence of an actual wooden equine has ever been found. Although Turkey has constructed a pretty fantastic facsimile for tourists.

Modern wisdom loudly proclaims: YOLO (You Only Live Once). But what if we don't? What if there's much more beyond this life, beyond what we can even dream or imagine? Truth is, I can't offer you concrete proof of heaven. I can only offer faith in what Scripture and God's Spirit whispers to me, what my heart declares is true: we were made for more. If that's true, when the Trojan Hearse arrives, how do we make a graceful exit?

REALITY CHECK, PLEASE

"What did I ever do to God to deserve this?" Mardel demanded, as though I had the authority to speak for the Almighty.

"Had the privilege of living more than ninety years?" I replied softly—half-question, half-answer, only half-hoping she'd hear.

My grandmother was in excellent health. Well, excellent health for someone whose body had almost a century's worth of living worn into it. I didn't mean to make light of her frustration. Getting old can be hard. It's hard to move, hard to sleep, hard to remember, and hard to watch your peers disappear one by one as the years go by. But I couldn't help thinking of so many of my friends whose lives seemed to have been cut short, who never had the chance to enjoy senior citizen discounts. Believe me, I had some questions for God as well.

Our timelines may differ, but we're all heading toward the same foregone conclusion. Regardless of how much we exercise, how low our cholesterol count, how consistently we wear sunscreen, or how positive our outlook on life may be, we're all going to die one day. It doesn't matter if we accept it or fear it, fight it or prepare for it, there's not one thing we can do to stop it. And we have no idea how far away, or how near, that moment is.

The hope of heaven doesn't negate the travail of death. After all, God Himself doesn't take death lightly. Psalm 116:15 says, "Precious in the sight of the Lord is the death of His saints" (NKJV). And the shortest verse in the Bible, "Jesus wept" (John 11:35 NKJV) records Jesus' reaction when he visits the tomb of his good friend Lazarus, a man Jesus would raise from the dead moments later. Still, Jesus was moved to tears.

Considering all of the emotional, theological, and eternal implications we have to ponder concerning our transition from life to death, I find it fascinating that one of the topics we spend the most time and thought on (not to mention expense) boils down to a question best suited to an episode of *CSI*: What should we do with the body?

My husband and I began, and finished, this discussion years ago. We decided to donate our bodies to science, where they could be used at a teaching hospital for medical research. This feels like responsible recycling. It also serves as an incentive to stay in shape. We figure this may help reduce the chance of students giving us nicknames like Tubby the Prune Princess or Jabba the What.

Grandma Mardel's main concern was that my sister and I find her a casket that had angels on each corner. She explained that without them, the real angels in heaven couldn't open her casket and she'd be stuck. And no, Mardel was not suffering from dementia at this time. Don't ask me where this theory came from. All I know is that Mardel was very, very serious about it. Unfortunately, my sister and I couldn't locate an angel-clad coffin. Sorry, Grandma. We tried.

For those with less eccentric tastes (which some might label "tasteless"), a woodworker in Maine creates coffins that double as coffee tables or entertainment centers. Use them now, be buried in them later. Or we can go to Holy-Smoke.com and have our cremated remains loaded into shotgun shells or rifle cartridges. Then our relatives can use them for target practice or hunting. It seems the human mind is never at a loss for ways to make a buck, even when it comes to our eventual demise.

Perhaps we put so much thought into what to do with our body because that's the last detail we feel we can control. The rest of death, like God Himself, is ultimately cloaked in mystery. We get hints of what heaven may be like from Scripture. John's vision in Revelation talks about bizarre-looking angelic beings, incense made of prayer, and streets of gold. Saint Brigid had a vision where heaven was a giant lake of beer. Who knows for sure? Like trying to describe our infinitely unfathomable God, life after death is just as likely to be beyond the scope of our limited vocabulary and human mind.

Personally, I find Steve Jobs' final words best capture my heart concerning our transition from life to death. He whispered, "Oh, wow … oh, wow … oh, wow." We have no idea what he was referring to. But I feel those words could be my mantra about life. Why not death?

A TALE OF TWO BIDDIES: THE SEQUEL

We were late. As usual. Getting two small children and one grandmother with dementia ready for a day out always took longer than planned. The kids pleaded to have Grandma Kitty sit in the backseat with them, but she was already seated in the front. Did I mention we were late? The *Muppets Christmas Movie* wouldn't wait to start just for us.

All it took was one small misstep getting out of the car. Kitty usually waited for me to unbuckle her seatbelt, but not today. Why not today? Why hadn't I taken the time to seat her in the back with the kids? And why, oh why do we have to grow old?

A broken hip quickly led to pneumonia. But the doctors assured me Kitty was recovering nicely. So our family decided to go ahead with our plans to spend Easter weekend up in the mountains, playing in the snow.

On our way out of town, we stopped by the hospital for a visit. "We'll be gone for a couple of days," I explained, "but we'll see you on Easter!"

"If I don't see you, have a happy Easter!" she replied.

"No, Grandma," I tried to explain, "we'll see you on Easter. We'll be back by then."

With a huge grin on her face and a wave of her thin, wrinkled hand, she repeated, "If I don't see you, have a happy Easter!" I shook my head at the toll dementia had taken as we headed off on our family adventure.

Kitty died the next day on Good Friday. Just like her beloved Savior. Every Easter since then, her last words and a picture of her sharing tea with Jesus, playfully bantering over the reality of what it means to rise again, comes to mind. Perhaps Kitty was aware of much more than I gave her credit for.

Six weeks after Kitty died, Grandma Mardel arrived. Time to put my caregiver's apron back on and get to work. And what character-building work it was! Six exasperating years later, I sat by Mardel's bedside, this time very aware that this grandmother's life on earth would likely be measured in days, if not hours. Although Mardel wasn't alert, I decided to read aloud, hoping she could hear my voice. What better words to read to someone like Mardel than her very own.

Back in the 1930s when Mardel was a young mother, she'd filled notebooks with original poetry. To help her increasingly confused memory try and find solid ground, I'd put together a scrapbook of her poems paired with old family photos. When I gave it to her, she'd chastised me for having the gall to give her a book with "obscene man parts" on the cover. The "man parts" were actually drawings of fruit. I grabbed the offending fruit book and started to read:

There's a tiny boat in the harbor with room for
    only one,
Waiting there for me when my work on earth
    is done.
I'll softly raise the anchor and hoist the sails
    up high
And gently leave the shore, waving my last unseen
    good-bye.
And when I enter a harbor where they who've
    gone before
Will reach out helping hands to pull my boat up
    on the shore,
I'll place my foot upon the sands where ever more
    I'll roam
Safe in my peaceful harbor, safe in my heavenly
    home!

My grandmother's poetry was filled with images of heaven and God's faithfulness, the blessings of family, and the simple joys of life. As I read Mardel's words, I thought, "Here's a woman I would have loved to have known." I wondered how and why she'd chosen to live her final years in a rut that drew her farther away from God, from those who tried to love her, and from the amazing woman she'd apparently been, someone who seemed at one time to have found faith, hope, and love so close at hand.

A Tale of Two Biddies doesn't end here. It's still being written in heaven and continues being penned through you and me here on earth. What kind of story will our Biddy Years tell? What ruts will we choose to travel or leave behind? Will we choose life or death, blessings or curses? That decision lies with you and me. Up until the time we board that "tiny boat in the harbor" or whatever means of travel our journey toward eternity takes, there's still time to reinvent ourselves. Let's use that fleeting time well.

And if, perchance, our paths should cross in heaven, I have one request. If the angels haven't yet figured out how to free Mardel, would you help me get her out?